love letters

FROM THE MuM

Dear Amanda,

Keep your faith

Work for others to be

an overrayal.

Always,

Love,

Peace & Joy?!,

J. Cully-Burns

love letters
FROM THE MuM

Gwendolyn Cody-Davis

NOMOLAC, LLC

Printed in the United States of America
First Printing, 2020
ISBN: 978-1-7346793-0-4
Published by:
NOMOLAC LLC.

Editor: Jen West Writing Editing & Marketing Services
Editor: Greg Baker Affordable Christian Editing
Cover Photos: Kim Brundage Photography
Interior Formatting: Wendi Hayman Publishing Services
Cover Design: Dzine By Kellie

Unless otherwise noted, all scriptures are from the KING JAMES VERSION (KJV): KING JAMES VERSION, public domain.

Scripture taken from the New King James Version®. Copyright ©1982 by Thomas Nelson. Used by permission. All rights reserved.

Scriptures marked NIV are taken from the NEW INTERNATIONAL VERSION (NIV): Scripture is taken from THE HOLY BIBLE, NEW INTERNATIONAL VERSION ®. Copyright© 1973, 1978, 1984, 2011 by Biblica, Inc.™. Used by permission of Zondervan.

Scriptures marked TM is taken from the Biblical MESSAGE: THE BIBLE IN CONTEMPORARY ENGLISH (TM): Scripture taken from THE MESSAGE: THE BIBLE IN CONTEMPORARY ENGLISH, copyright©1993, 1994, 1995, 1996, 2000, 2001, 2002. Used by permission of NavPress Publishing Group.

Scripture quotations marked (NLT) are taken from the Holy Bible, New Living Translation, copyright ©1996, 2004, 2007 by Tyndale House Foundation. Used by permission of Tyndale House Publishers, a Division of Tyndale House Ministries, Carol Stream, Illinois 60188. All rights reserved.

Special SIBLINGS SHOUT OUT

I have lots of love and sweet memories of my oldest sister Jewelry, who often spoke of writing a book.
Love to my only brother, Booker T., aka Butch, and my baby sister, Tangela, aka Nisee.

And now
abideth
faith,
hope,
charity,
these three;
but the greatest of these
is charity.

1 Corinthians 13:1

Dedication

Dear Ryan and Reagan,

Though you are young adults now, I am still explaining lessons learned from your great grandmother, Marie Cody. Lessons about life, and the Lord God, who created you. I am presenting these lessons to you through candid conversations while trying my best to live the life of a Christian wife and mum.

Your Dad and I trained you to love God, and always remember He is first in your life. The answers to all of life's questions are in the Bible, God's most excellent love letter. Use it wisely.

Praise is one of your most powerful weapons. You were taught very early in life how to praise the Lord, how to live a life of worship, and the importance of being a covenant baby. From a very young age, you were tithers. Continue in this principal, and you will prosper.

Keep this information forever engrafted in your hearts and be sure to pass it on to your children, grandchildren and great grandchildren. Be a great example to the people that the Lord places in your path.

Much love and respect, "Ma, MuM"

Dedicated TO MY FAMILY TREE

What a joyous thrill for me
To pass down rituals, heirlooms, and history
To my present and future family tree
It's more than a privilege to leave this legacy

Precious daughters and priest of homes' sons
March to the beat of your drum
But listen to these words of wisdom from my heart
Family heritage is rich in these parts

Beloved, keep these letters deep within your spirit
Life is a combination of highs and lows
But keep God first, and you will never have to worry
As you walk in ordered steps, thank Him for opened doors

Love,
"the MuM"

TABLE OF CONTENTS

FOREWORD...1
TRIBUTE...2
INTRODUCTION...3
LETTER ONE...7
Faith Over Fear
LETTER TWO..15
Giving and Receiving God's Love
LETTER THREE.......................................25
Family Legacy
LETTER FOUR...39
Into Each Life Some Rain Must Fall
LETTER FIVE..50
Be Yourself
LETTER SIX..59
Living on the Positive Side of Life…
LETTER SEVEN......................................67
Your Gifts, Talents, and Abilities
LETTER EIGHT..76
Purpose
LETTER NINE...84
Destiny Moments

LETTER TEN...93
It Was the Best of Times and the Worst of Times
LETTER ELEVEN...................................102
Spiritual House Cleaning
LETTER TWELVE...................................109
Light Over Darkness
LETTER THIRTEEN................................118
How to Be an Encourager
LETTER FOURTEEN................................124
Think Before You Speak, and Speak in Love
LETTER FIFTEEN...................................134
Have You Ever Felt Like a Nobody?
LETTER SIXTEEN...................................141
What a Difference a Day Makes
LETTER SEVENTEEN..............................145
You Can Do It Too; It All Starts with You
Epilogue...151
Acknowledgments..................................152
About the Author...................................154
Girly Girly...156
Dreams...157
Goals...160

Foreword

There is always something that warms my heart when I am in the presence of a person of grace and nobility. The author of this book has those qualities. MuM is a perfect description of Elder Gwendolyn Cody-Davis, a servant of God that radiates smiles and happiness to everyone she meets. This book will allow you to feel the love and compassion of one of God's most encouraging servants.

Over a decade ago, the Lord impressed upon my heart to call her Esther—I can definitely see why! Gwendolyn Cody-Davis is a modern-day Queen Esther in the kingdom of God. She has a radiance about her that lets you know you are in the presence of one that is anointed to encourage. She uplifts the people of God, in the kingdom of God, for such a time as this! God has gifted her with a very heart-warming gift of encouragement.

The chrysanthemum ("mum") is known for its ability to bring happiness and smiles to the faces of others. When you smile, you are radiating to others the heart of God. Elder Gwendolyn Cody-Davis has not only written a book, but she has injected her spirit of grace and nobility into each and every page.

As you read this book, you will smile often, but you will also feel the love of God, encouraging you to live with joy and enthusiasm each day, regardless of life's circumstances.

-Bishop C.E. Wiley

1

Tribute

In 2001, my mother, Thelma L. Cody, sent a few books in the mail to me. They were Baptist Training Union (BTU) books that once belonged to my grandmother, Marie Cody. She was the director of BTU in our church for many years. With those books, my mother had this note: Share these books with Ryan and Reagan (ages 11 and 6 at the time); tell them about your grandmother and help them understand the lessons.

Introduction

The grass withers, the flower fades, But the word of our God stands forever.
Isaiah 40:8 NKJV

I love flowers. I did not believe I had the green thumb that my mother has nor the green thumb that my aunt had for many years. But I love flowers and plants because they have a unique energy. Flowers can illuminate, and they bring much delight.

The chrysanthemums, nicknamed mums, were first used as a flowering herb. This flower is so popular that the Japanese celebrate a national chrysanthemum day called the Festival of Happiness. Imagine celebrating a flower to help bring smiles and joy to others. If all it takes is flowers, we all need to become gardeners because there are many faces that need smiles.

I was first introduced to the chrysanthemum as a corsage worn at homecoming football games. The most widely grown potted plant in the country to this day, as well as one of the longest lasting of all cut flowers, is, of course, mums.

Maybe you have noticed how the chrysanthemum makes a beautiful fall display for the home garden as well as an excellent landscaping plant. You cannot go wrong with growing chrysanthemums.

Traditionally, the bloom of this flower signals the arrival of the Fall season, but I've come to appreciate a deeper pronouncement—a time of change. It's as if there's a season of change that's not dictated by a calendar. It's both exhilarating and transformative in that; this change ushers me into a brand-new horizon of spiritual growth.

Over the years, I have become a great gardener. At my last job, several colleagues nicknamed me "the plant nurse." They would bring their "already-on-life support" plants for me to nurse back to health. I nurtured these plants back to life with proper sunlight, plant food, water, and of course, tender loving care. Some of these plants beautify my home today.

The first key lesson I learned in life is to put in the hard work, go after your dreams, and don't be afraid to get your fingernails dirty in the process. This lesson learned sticks with me to this day. The old saying that the apple doesn't fall far from the tree must be true. Thanks, MuDear, and thanks, Aunt Charlie Mae.

Why Am I, "MuM?" It's All in the Name

In my eyes, the world became a better place on February 17, 1990, and again on February 10, 1995. Those were the days—my husband and I—became parents to our two kings, Ryan and Reagan. I so vividly remember on February 16, 1990, leaving our Bowie, Maryland, home, heading to Walter Reed Army Hospital in Washington, D.C. looking back at our townhome and saying simultaneously, "our lives will never be the same." We just didn't know exactly how much things would change, but things would change in a good way, right?

After nine years of being Mr. and Mrs., a little person was about to enter the world and into our lives. Through this little one would come so much joy, and the parenting role would bring so much excitement as well as responsibility. The same thing would happen again in Naples, Italy, five years later, when our second king arrived.

The first name our oldest son called me was "MiMi." I have that name on hold to be used again in the future. Maybe. As he got older, Ryan called me "Ma." He still does to this day. Our youngest son, Reagan, calls me "MuM." I love both names. I am known as the Queen MuM. So, there you have it! The name is not original. I am.

Why Love Letters?

In this busy, digital age, we very seldom receive letters any longer from anyone, especially love letters. Each chapter of this book is a letter describing my real-life experiences reflected by my effervescent personality and the promises of God executed through the pages of His Holy Word. These letters are to be passed down to the generations to come—as well as to you—my beloveds.

How to Use This Book

At the end of each letter, I offer self-exam questions. Take your time to ponder each one. As you do, I hope your thoughts will lead to the answers you have been seeking. I pose the questions to help you assess where you are—and more importantly—where you hope to be relative to the given topic. I encourage you to pray and partner with the Lord through the Holy Spirit on how to get you there.

Just before the famous quotes that close each letter, I've inserted faith confessions. Our confession of faith will help seal the deal. I strongly encourage you to say them aloud. I believe there's tremendous power in a spoken confession. I consider these to be affirmations of faith spoken out of your mouth into the atmosphere. You are what you say you are, and you will have what you say you will have.

"If you would be happy for a lifetime, grow
Chrysanthemums."
-A Chinese philosopher

Letter One

FAITH OVER FEAR

For God has not given us a spirit of fear, but of power and of love and of a sound mind.
2 Timothy 1:7 NKJV

Dear Beloved,

Faith is a small five letter word, but when used effectively, it can move mountains. Without it, you are unable to progress in God's original design and purpose for your life. In Romans 10:17 we are told, "So then faith cometh by hearing, and hearing by the word of God." Are you listening to narratives that build up your faith to live out your God-given purpose, or are you listening to information that will keep you in a permanent state of fear?

I began my college education at age 42. The decision to do so proved to be one of the most profound eye-opening experiences this girl could have. It has served as a great confidence booster for my life's mission. I will always be grateful for adult education programs. This one was tailor-made just for me because it allowed me to wear many hats—wife, parent, employee, and student—simultaneously.

I learned, most of all, how to think critically, speak publicly, and write effectively—three mega-skills very much needed in today's society. I will expound on the public speaking aspect in a later letter.

Being a student helped to shape me in ways I could not have imagined. When I think about the experience, I wondered why it took me so long to begin my collegiate journey. In a word—fear. What caused me to fear? Fear of failure, a lack of self-esteem, and a lack of self-confidence. Who knew? Most people who know me would not have detected that inadequacy in me. I now realize that fear prevents so many people from taking steps of faith, thus stalling new ventures from ever being explored and ambitions and dreams from ever being fulfilled.

Every time I visit a cemetery or pass by one, I think of all of the gifts, skills, and talents that never materialized because of fear of failure. Failure is a lack or deficiency of a desirable quality. But keep in mind that failure does not have to represent a lack of something needed to succeed. The best people in their respective fields have failed at something, and some failed more than once. But what they were able to do was use their failures to achieve success. The truth of the matter is that failure is inevitable, and actually, failure leads to success in so many instances.

We define fear in many ways. Some describe it as a very unpleasant emotion that inflicts pain, fright, the anticipation of danger, and terror. Fear alone is an adversary to human progress. It keeps us from finishing the present and advancing into the future. Fear tends to keep us small, quiet, and apprehensive. If you're not careful, a spirit of fear will grip you so tightly you'll forget that the promises of God are for you and your family.

The believer is quick to make the declaration that the Lord did not give us the spirit of fear. But if the truth "be told," we all have scary moments. The key is not to allow a moment to turn into a day and a day into a week.

The Word of God comes to the rescue as we read and meditate on it and submit ourselves to prayer. God's Word reassures us that we can make it—if we try. Trusting in God and His Holy Word allows us to combat every ounce of fear. As previously mentioned, fear is an adversary, and it cannot exist with faith.

I will be the first to admit that there is an ounce of doubt that we sometimes experience. It's not that you do not believe in God or that you do not believe in yourself; it's that all humans have an ounce of doubt that we seem to have trouble extracting. If you do the research, you will find that doubt is a close relative of fear.

The Word of the Lord provides you with hope and comfort in your scary moments. Deuteronomy 31:8 lets you know that the Lord goes before you, He will be with you, and there is no failure in Him. Most assuredly, we can rely upon the faithfulness of the Lord.

Envision God's benevolence. Permit His comfort and strength to overtake you. Switch-on your spiritual ears and listen to David's song as recorded in Psalm 18:2. The psalmist declares, "The LORD is my rock, and my fortress, and my deliverer; my God, my strength, in whom I will trust; my buckler, and the horn of my salvation, and my high tower."

There are probably not many people in your life that you can refer to as a rock. Just for a moment, consider the imagery and symbolism of a rock. Solid. Unchanging. Dependable. Supportive. Substantial. People change, but God never changes. People disappoint, but God never disappoints. He is, hands down, the same yesterday, today, and forever. If God says He has your back, what do you have to fear?

Psalm 27 provides much confidence and courage, and

this psalm is my youngest son's absolute favorite passage in the Bible:

The LORD is my light and my salvation; whom shall, I fear? The LORD is the strength of my life; of whom shall I be afraid?

When the wicked, even mine enemies and my foes, came upon me to eat up my flesh, they stumbled and fell.

Though a host should encamp against me, my heart shall not fear: though war should rise against me, in this will I be confident.

One thing have I desired of the LORD, that will I seek after; that I may dwell in the house of the LORD all the days of my life, to behold the beauty of the LORD, and to enquire in His temple.

For in the time of trouble He shall hide me in His pavilion: in the secret of His tabernacle shall He hide me; He shall set me up upon a rock.

And now shall mine head be lifted up above mine enemies' round about me: therefore, will I offer in His tabernacle sacrifices of joy; I will sing, yea, I will sing praises unto the LORD.

Hear, O LORD, when I cry with my voice: have mercy also upon me, and answer me.

When thou sadist, seek ye my face; my heart said unto thee, thy face, LORD, will I seek.

Hide not thy face far from me; put not thy servant away in anger: thou hast been my help; leave me not,

neither forsake me, O God of my salvation.
When my father and my mother forsake me, then the
LORD will take me up.

Teach me thy way, O LORD, and lead me in a plain
path, because of mine enemies.

Deliver me not over unto the will of mine enemies:
for false witnesses are risen up against me, and such
as breathe out cruelty.

I had fainted, unless I had believed to see the goodness
of the LORD in the land of the living.

Wait on the LORD: be of good courage, and He shall
strengthen thine heart: wait, I say, on the LORD.

Faith is always present tense. In Hebrews 11:1-2, the writer reminds us, "Now faith is the substance of things hoped for, the evidence of things not seen. For by it, the elders obtained a good report."

How many times have you heard the saying that many can talk the talk, but few can walk the walk—the faith walk? Faith walkers are also over-comers. It sounds really great to talk about faith. You may feel as if it makes you look super spiritual to say you are a faith walker. But when the Pastor gives the benediction in church, and you have to return to your real-world, (your home, your family, your friends, your enemies, your job, your community, your space, your dreams, and your drama), how will you continue to walk in faith?

There comes a time in life when you must put your faith into action. You cannot just pray for it and never plan to use it. God has provided instructions in the Word on what the faith fight is all about.

First Timothy 6:12 (NKJV) says, "Fight the good fight of faith, lay hold on eternal life, to which you were also called and have confessed the good confession in the presence of many witnesses."

I can hear my Bishop saying emphatically, *"We're fighting from a place of victory."* You do know we win, right?

We experience so many changing times and seasons in our lives. For instance, the Coronavirus is one of those seasons no one saw coming. The entire pandemic brought on so much fear, which I liken to the speed of a rollercoaster ride. At times, we felt like we were on top of the mountain. Then, other times with exceptional speed, we felt we were racing to the bottom of the hill. In descending times, remember fear has to bow, torment has to surrender, and doubt has to bounce. They certainly cannot remain in the presence of a faithful God.

Love,
"the MuM"

Self - Exam Questions

1. What is meant by the statement, "Walking by faith and not by sight?"
2. Is there a need to increase my faith in my life? If so, how will I accomplish this task?
3. How can Hebrews 11:6 help me on my faith journey?
4. What do I do when fear seems insurmountable?

Faith Confessions

I decree and declare that according to St. Luke 1:30, fear cannot rule in my life because I have favor with God. I decree and declare that I walk by faith and not by sight. I stand on God's Word that never fails, and according to Romans 8:28, "And we know that all things work together for good to those who love God, to those who are the called according to His purpose." I stand on God's Word that never fails, and according to Philippians 4:13, "I can do all things through Christ who strengthens me." I stand on God's Word that never fails, and according to St. Matthew 17:20, it only takes mustard seed faith to speak to the mountain and watch it move, and nothing shall be impossible for me.

"The greatest test of courage on earth is to bear defeat without losing heart."
-Robert Green Ingersoll

Letter Two

GIVING AND RECEIVING GOD'S LOVE

For God so loved the world that he gave his one and only
Son, that whoever believes in him shall not perish but
have eternal life.
St. John 3:16 NIV

Dear Beloved,

Guess what? I have a special invitation just for you. Generally speaking, who wouldn't love to receive an invitation? There's something about receiving one that I'm sure makes you feel special. When someone invites you to an event or gathering, it adds to your sense of inclusion. Well, I want to extend the greatest invitation you could ever expect to receive while on earth. If you have not already made the most important decision you will ever make, you can certainly make it right here, and right now. This invitation is to God's salvation. It tops your financial choices, your investment determinations, and your business decisions. Once the decision is made to accept the Lord into your life, you're in the winner's circle here on earth and in eternal life as well.

Understandably, you have your set of priorities. However, it is crucial not only to be concerned with your physical life events but also to ensure your spiritual being is well-maintained. You need to have a plan of action.

By the way, have you reviewed any plans lately? Such as your life insurance policy, health plan, auto, home insurance, 401K, or a business plan? The primary goal for the researcher is benefits. Even when applying for positions in your career, benefits are usually on your list of priorities. Psalm 68:19 (NKJV) informs us, "Blessed *be* the Lord, *Who* daily loads us *with benefits*, The God of our salvation! *Selah*." That's worthy of a praise break right there because, not only is the salvation plan sufficient to save you, but daily, the Lord still comes through for you.

Have you considered "Eternal Life Insurance?" The word "insure" means a guarantee of compensation for specified loss, damage, illness, or death in return for the payment of a premium. The premium protects against a possible negative eventuality. There's one thing to note about eternal life insurance. There's no premium because Jesus prepaid it. Jesus died on Calvary's cross just to guarantee your salvation. Additionally, the Bible teaches about your natural state of how you entered the world. Psalm 51:5 (NIV) says, "Surely I was sinful at birth, sinful from the time my mother conceived me."

Realize that you are not perfect, and when you fail, you can and should repent and get right back up with absolutely no condemnation. You entered this world with a sinful nature. No one had to teach you how to take a cookie from the cookie jar and lie to your mother about it.

To simplify it even further, pretend you are editing a 150-page document, you've made significant changes, but somehow, you missed clicking the "save" button. Sad. Oh, what a tragic and costly mistake. With one keystroke, your revisions vanish with little chance of recovering them.

If you hear the salvation story, find that it is beneficial to you, and accept Jesus as your Lord and Savior, it's as if the Lord clicks the "save" button for your soul. Methodically, a new document is created called "new life" for each individual that accepts the invitation. It also places you as part of the universal Body of Christ, and it makes you and I family—brothers and sisters.

There are two things most people have in common. You are physically born, and you grow up. As you journey through life hopefully someone will introduce you to the plan of salvation that assures everlasting life. Not everyone receives an invitation to this *kind* of party, so I am taking the time to extend a simple invitation just for you.

Maybe you have started reading this book, and while you cannot wait to get to the good part, you have landed on this question and became uncomfortable and ready to move on to another letter. To me this is the best part of the book because it is so important.

There are several benefits to being saved, such as salvation puts us at peace with God. There's another question to examine. Why should I want to be saved?

Therefore, having been justified by faith, we have peace with God through our Lord Jesus Christ.
- Romans 5:1

And guess what? You are no longer an enemy of God.

For if, while we were God's enemies, we were reconciled to him through the death of his Son, how much more, having been reconciled, shall we be saved through his life!
- Romans 5:10 (NIV)

It is a good thing to be saved; it simply means that you place your full trust in the Lord Jesus Christ, and you know that He's forgiven your sins. Knowing this, who wouldn't want to be saved?

For I delivered unto you first of all that which I also received, how that Christ died for our sins according to the scriptures; And that he was buried, and that he rose again the third day according to the scriptures.
- 1 Corinthians 15:3-4

The Bible also lets you know:

And these will go away into everlasting punishment, but the righteous into eternal life.
- St. Matthew 25:46 NKJV

Just in case you are not aware, there's another benefit. We live for eternity. In other words, why spend time worrying about death when you know you're going to live forever?

There is one essential truth to keep in mind. After you accept the Lord into your heart, I highly encourage you to find a local church, get plugged in, continue to grow, continue to be blessed, and become a blessing to many others.

If this is the first time you have seriously considered the need for Christ in your life, all you have to do is realize that everyone has fallen short, made mistakes, and sinned, and also realize redemption is necessary. You can accept Jesus in your heart, put your faith in Him, and receive His grace. Thus, a brand-new life has begun.

After you have accepted the Lord into your life, the truth is, you will still make mistakes. You will sometimes fall short; however, it is with the new mindset that you now genuinely know how to repent, ask for forgiveness, receive God's forgiveness, and move on. That makes you a winner, and you are certainly on the right team— the winning team.

Then comes the time to share your faith with others. It's called soul winning. What exactly is winning souls? It's sharing your testimony. It's really just like anything else. For example, when you share a very positive experience regarding your real estate agent, your car salesperson, your mechanic, your trainer, your hairstylist, or your nail technician with others, they usually want the same experience, right? Of course, they do. When you share the goodness of the Lord with others who don't have a personal relationship with Him, the results should be the same. Someone—although maybe not everyone—should want that relationship as well.

This question has been asked in our ministry in Prince George, Virginia, for the last few years, especially at the beginning of almost every new year, how many souls will you win for the Lord this year? It is a rhetorical question; however, indeed, it is one to be contemplated. I figured out that there is only one person that can answer this question, and that person is me. I have concluded that, from this book, I would step out on crazy faith to ask you the very same question. How many souls will you win for the Lord this year?

The business world is hugely metric-oriented. Businesses rely on metrics to measure or track progress made toward achieving a specific benchmark or initiative. We should have a great concern for metrics as it relates to souls as well. At the end of the day, if you witness and display the love of God, heaven's population should be much higher than hell's population. But for that to be true statistically, the passion for soul winning has to start with us. Beloved, heaven, is real. We find these words in scripture:

In My Father's house are many mansions; if it were not so, I would have told you. I go to prepare a place for you. And if I go and prepare a place for you, I will come again and receive you to Myself; that where I am, there you may be also.
- St. John 14:2-3

It is not the most popular subject, but hell is also a very real place prepared for the devil and his angels, according to St. Matthew 25:41.

So, set a goal not to allow anyone or anything to come between your soul and your Savior—not a spouse, a child, a parent, or a career. Emphatically, nothing should come between you and your relationship with your Lord.

You can help others become soul winners too. As followers of Christ, you also need to be prepared to share the message of the gospel at any time. Wouldn't you just love to be the bearer of good news for a change? You will not run across this invitation on MSNBC, CNN, or on the local news; however, it is breaking news, nevertheless. It is the gospel of Jesus Christ. The word "gospel" means "good news"—the good news of Jesus Christ, our Savior.

The following principles are very basics, but they are useful when sharing the plan of salvation with others. Just realize how much God loves the world and just how much He wants to have a personal relationship with each person. You were made for relationships. Let's tell the whole world. Are you ready for basic training? Let's go.

There is a simple way to lead people to Jesus. It is commonly called "The Romans Road," which is a series of scriptures from the book of Romans that some use in presenting the gospel. Since the gospel literally means good news, it's exciting to invite others to Christ. Just as a military recruiter takes pride in new recruits, the Bible tells you that the angels in heaven rejoice over one soul.

Just so people will not think for a minute that they must have it all together to be saved, you can share Romans 3:10 which says, "As it is written, there is none righteous, not one." Jesus is the only righteous one, and He can help you get into a position to meet God.

You can also share with others that everyone has done wrong. Romans 3:23 says, "For all have sinned, and come short of the glory of God." Romans 6:23 says, "For the wages of sin is death; but the gift of God is eternal life through Jesus Christ our Lord."

I am so impressed with the fact that God didn't wait for me to get—as some say— "cleaned up" before I received salvation; Lord knows, I couldn't have done it. The great news is that if you allow Him, He can, and He will. Romans 5:8 tells us, "But God commendeth His love toward us, in that, while we were yet sinners, Christ died for us." You can also share:

But when the kindness and love of God our Savior toward man appeared, not by works of righteous which we have done, but according to His mercy He saved us, through the washing of regeneration and renewing of the Holy Spirit.
- Titus 3:4-5 NKJV

Yet to all who receive him, to those who believed in His name, he gave the right to become children of God.
- St. John 1:12 NIV

Through thick and thin, keep your hearts at attention, in adoration before Christ, your Master. Be ready to speak up and tell anyone who asks why you're living the way you are, and always with the utmost courtesy.
- 1 Peter 3:15 TM

Christ's life showed me how, and enabled me to do it. I identified myself completely with him. Indeed, I have been crucified with Christ. My ego is no longer central. It is no longer important that I appear righteous before you or have your good opinion, and I am no longer driven to impress God. Christ lives in me. The life you see me living is not "mine," but it is lived by faith in the Son of God, who loved me and gave himself for me.
- Galatians 2:20 TM

You can't pick and choose in these things, specializing

in keeping one or two things in God's law and ignoring others.
- James 2:10 TM

All we like sheep have gone astray; we have turned every one to his own way, and the LORD hath laid on him the iniquity of us all.
- Isaiah 53:6

We love him, because He first loved us.
- 1 John 4:19

If you have not already done so, consider making salvation a priority. Even when going through persecution, as explained in Revelation 2:10b, consider the crown of life as your reward. The crown of life is a special honor, reward, or recognition given by Jesus to those who stand up against the temptations and trials of the enemy.

The crown is the reward to the faithful for being just that— faithful. Crowns are defined as types of headgear worn by a monarch as a symbol of sovereignty, often made of precious metal and ornamented with valuable gems. The ancients conferred it as a mark of victory or as an athletic or military distinction.

The most important thing to remember is to stay the course, be strong in the Lord and in the power of His might, remain faithful, and determined to make a difference.

Love,
"the MuM"

Self - Exam Questions:

1. In listing my priorities, what is the most critical life decision I could ever make?
2. How comfortable am I to share my faith with others?
3. What would it take to bring me out of my comfort zone when it comes to soul winning?

Faith Confessions

I declare by faith that I have confessed with my mouth and have believed in my heart that God has raised Jesus from the dead, and because of my confession of faith, the Bible says I am saved. I declare by faith that I am justified, just as if I have never sinned. I declare by faith that I am the righteousness of God in Christ Jesus. I am delighted to be in the family of God.

"When you arise in the morning, think of what a precious privilege it is to be alive to breathe, to think, to enjoy, to love."
-Marcus Aurelius

Letter Three

FAMILY LEGACY

Don't you see that children are GOD'S best gift?
The fruit of the womb is his generous legacy?
Like a warrior's fistful of arrows are the children of a
vigorous youth. Oh, how blessed are you parents, with
your quivers full of children!
Your enemies don't stand a chance against you; you'll
sweep them right off your doorstep.
Psalm 127:3-5 TM

Dear Beloved,

Let the positive life cycle continue. Have you considered that each generation should be encouraged to get better than the previous one? Not just for the sake of outshining your parents or your grandparents. However, it is exciting to witness when it comes to evolving and improving the family structure. It is an absolute blessing for parents to see their children use their gifts, talents, and abilities and watch them go to the next dimension. It speaks volumes to the legacy of the family.

I am privileged to be a part of a ministry where the seed principle is taught and emphasized over and over. I didn't realize just how powerful the seed principle was until I began to put those lessons into practice. Believe me—the Word becomes a part of you when you put it into practice.

It is definitely part of the essential plan of God to expect a harvest after a seed is planted. Seeds reproduce after its kind. So, you should not expect to receive a crop of apricots after a plum seed is sown.

I didn't grow up on a farm; however, I find it very interesting to talk with people who have, or to read, or even watch programs regarding farm life. When I think about a farmer, I think about duties that are involved in maintaining a farm. Taking care of the livestock, driving tractors, and general handiwork are all critical. Still, to me, the actual planting and harvesting crops are the most exciting responsibilities for a farmer. Sowing seed and putting in all the hard work makes the harvest just that much more exhilarating.

Spiritually speaking, the seed is the Word of God. It is God's Word that brings about changed lives. The Bible says the (spiritual) sower sows the Word of God in St. Mark 4:1-9. The Word, as a spiritual seed, needs a ready heart to receive and incubate so it can bear fruit. It is the Word as a seed that gets people born again.

Consistent growth from the elementary principle of Christ, from the milk of the Word to the meat of the Word, quickly moves us from being babes to being teachers of the Word. The Bible lets us know in 1 Peter 1:23 as well as 1 John 3:9 that this is the Word that conceived the new life in you.

Just as seeds are essential to plants because they ensure that the gene pool will continue to the next generation, it is vital that parents, aunts, uncles, cousins—the entire village—positively contribute to the mindset of our youth. The village needs to let our young people know the enormity of the seed placed inside of them, and, just like a popular television show, we can sit back and stay tuned to a spinoff of greatness continuing generation after generation.

It does not matter if you are part of a one-parent family, two-parent family, or blended family; parents who genuinely love our children, and those who are in a position to do so, will do everything humanly possible to ensure that our children have the best lives. We want our children to have the best education, exposure to the things to be valued later in life, as well as exposure to the things that we did not have.

Godly parents also want to make sure that we are present and able to guide our children through the growing up years. Then, one day, parents graduate to become "consultants" to be there to provide advice if needed. What I have witnessed is, even if a parent lives long enough to see their child reach age 60 or 70 or beyond, they take special pride in being asked to provide guidance on matters of the children's concerns.

Parenting is not the easiest job in the world, primarily because we are living in difficult times. Most parents and guardians will admit, raising children like we were raised might not work as well today. However, there is one thing to keep at the forefront of your mind; love is one of the first things you should show and teach your child. Love will never become old fashioned. Children mimic what they see; so, if you operate in the spirit of love, it allows them to duplicate it.

This type of action lets the world know just who you are indeed. St. John 13:35 says, "By this shall all men know that ye are my disciples if ye have love one to another." When you display this type of parental or guardian love, you will have reached the hearts of many.

In other words, as a parent, your best gift to leave for the next generation is your love, wisdom, and godly examples. You probably have heard the saying, "experience is the best teacher." If that saying has any truth, you will find it very beneficial to use your experiences to help someone else, especially our youth.

Maybe you are not a parent, but perhaps you influence our youth through family, church, work, or in the community. As you share some of your experiences with them, keep in mind that some will listen, and some won't, but share the kind of lessons that you wish someone had taken the time to share with you.

Christian parents should also make it a priority to ensure that our children have a relationship with the Lord. From that relationship, everything else is built—love, joy, peace, faith, wisdom, compassion, and security.

As a child, I listened quite intensely to the information and stories shared by my elders. I didn't know it at the time that I was born to succeed. As I journeyed into adulthood, I gained a greater appreciation for all the wisdom instilled in me by the older generation.

I was born and raised in Thomasville, Georgia. I didn't realize it then, but I was so very blessed to be raised in a household with my dad, mother, paternal grandmother, as well as my youngest sister. When anyone asked my mother how many children she and my dad had, she would always respond by saying, "I have two home, and two gone on." At that time, I was the oldest one at home. My older siblings had already left home to make their mark in the world.

My dad, Charles T. Cody, was affectionately called by his initials, Mr. C.T. He was a World War II Veteran in the United States Navy, and after his years of service, he was an insurance agent, carpenter, and custodian. My dad spent a great deal of his career employed at the Board of Education as a custodian. He also was elated for the opportunity to pursue a part-time job as a bus driver for the athletic teams of our local high school, Thomasville High.

Though Dad welcomed the extra coins from his part-time gig, that was not the sole reason he was interested in this position. Dad was a lover of all sports. His favorites were baseball, football, basketball, and boxing, so he welcomed the opportunity because it was not like work to him at all.

I remember my grandmother counseling him on the issue. She asked my dad, "C.T., do you think this will be a little too much to do at night along with your full-time job, your family, and church?" It was maybe a couple of times a week, depending on the season. He assured her that this was the right decision and that he thought he would like it. Well, he did. That part-time position brought him into proximity to the coaches, players, and the administrative staff of the high school.

Dad looked up to the school secretary, and during those years (the 1970s), the secretary was often a female. The secretary was also the one that had my dad's paycheck for the part-time bus driver gig.

It became my job to stop by the office on his payday, before I left school, to collect his paycheck and bring it home to him.

When my youngest sister Tangela (Tan), and I started our careers after high school, we both became secretaries or part of the administrative staff of our respective organizations. Dad was excited for his daughters to experience the office environment because it was a position he valued so tremendously. Tan began her career at the Board of Education, our Dad's employer, for many years.

As a custodian, Dad used to make the white lines on the football field before the Friday night games. Little did my dad or any of us know, though he started at the custodian level, years later, two of his daughters would start their careers on administrative staff as secretaries. And over twenty years later, two of his grandsons would coach college football on the white lines that Dad (the barrier breaker), so graciously and faithfully marked on the football field. After our dad's initial retirement, he returned to work at the Board of Education, this time as a supervisor of the custodians.

When I realized the progression that had transpired in my family over three generations, it excited me. Even before ever receiving a prophecy or a vision to write this book, I mentioned this advancement to my mother, and she thought it was phenomenal. She even commented, "Only Gwen would make that connection."

The older I get, the more I am told that I look like my mother, and then again, it's all part of the seed principle. Like most Christian mothers, she taught me to treat people like I wanted to be treated, love others, and be a lady. She mentored me in public speaking at a very young age.

Easter time, as we called it, was a very festive time in our community. It was just as exciting as the Christmas season. Children would pack our church out to participate in the activities that led up to our annual Easter program and Easter egg hunt. We would have "Easter practice," which was just as exciting as the actual program, held at 6 p.m. on that Sunday evening at Willowhead Missionary Baptist Church. When I thought about it, I learned all the little kids' Easter speeches, along with my own, which my mom made sure was not a four-liner. I always had what I would call a lengthy speech somewhat, even as early as ages eight and nine. But it was effortless to learn because I had a photographic memory.

Not only did I have to memorize my speech, but I had to use the dynamics that my mom taught me as well as the appropriate gestures. I was taught not to rush it, but to make sure I made eye contact and expressed the words as if I was saying, "I was born for this."

Sure enough, one of my younger cousins forgot one of her lines one year. I remember her saying, "Easter is a time of joy," and the next words I heard were my mother saying,

"Tell her, Gwen," and I said, "For every little girl and boy," and of course, my cousin repeated it and received a round of applause.

Each child received praise. We didn't realize it at the time, but recognition for a child is significant because it helps to build self-confidence. The adults used to say, "We're going to give them a hand for coming to the stage, whether they remembered their speech or not."

Family legacy is essential. Think about it; family is God's most precious prized possession. You should want to leave a positive family legacy and not a negative one. As I reflect on my family, I am reminded of the first family. The first family I am referring to is the family who resided in the Garden of Eden.

After Adam and Eve made a costly mistake and sinned against God, they were forced out of their garden home. Then they began to be fruitful and multiply. Their firstborn, Cain, was a farmer, and the second son's name was Abel; his occupation was a shepherd. When it was time for sacrifices to be offered to God, Cain brought fruit from the ground, as an act of worship. Abel brought the fat portions from some of the firstborn sheep. God showed favor to Abel's sacrifice, but He didn't extend that same grace to Cain. This rejection made Cain angry, and God warned Cain to do the right thing so that his sacrifice would be accepted as well. The caveat was if Cain refused to do the right thing, it wouldn't be a satisfactory ending because sin was ready to consume him.

Instead of freely receiving God's instructions, Cain disregarded God's warning. He took out his anger on his innocent brother Abel. Cain invited Abel to come out to the fields where he murdered him. Later, God approached Cain about Abel's whereabouts. Cain lied and replied to the all-knowing God with the infamous question, perhaps one you have heard, "Am I my brother's keeper?"

God responded quickly with the pronouncement of His

punishment. Maybe you know the rest of the story. Genesis 4:11-17 informs us:

And now art thou cursed from the earth, which hath opened her mouth to receive thy brother's blood from thy hand;

When thou tillest the ground, it shall not henceforth yield unto thee her strength; a fugitive and a vagabond shalt thou be in the earth.

And Cain said unto the LORD, My punishment is greater than I can bear. Behold, thou hast driven me out this day from the face of the earth; and from thy face shall I be hid; and I shall be a fugitive and a vagabond in the earth; and it shall come to pass, that every one that findeth me shall slay me.

And the LORD said unto him, Therefore whosoever slayeth Cain, vengeance shall be taken on him sevenfold. And the LORD set a mark upon Cain, lest any finding him should kill him.

And Cain went out from the presence of the LORD, and dwelt in the land of Nod, on the east of Eden. And Cain knew his wife; and she conceived, and bare Enoch: and he builded a city, and called the name of the city, after the name of his son, Enoch.

The first family was not without dysfunction. This is the reason family members need to always be aware of the enemy's attributions, and his devices. His job specification is found in St. John 10:10a. It informs us that, "The thief cometh not, but for to steal, and to kill, and to destroy." He is a liar, murderer, and sower of discord; he is a cunning thief, and he is extremely evil. If ever there was a time for the family to stay on guard and stay in the presence of God, it is right now.

Perhaps you have heard we serve a God of second chances. Adam and Eve's story was not over. God blessed them with another son they called Seth. Eve's thoughts were that the Lord had appointed her another offspring in place of Abel, for Cain killed him. God has a way when it looks like it's all over, of allowing you to begin again.

Suppose you are a soldier on the battlefield in the army of the Lord, report for duty. If you don't, the enemy will destroy your family, your life, and all the important things and people you value and hold so dear.

In 1 Peter 5:8 we were told, "Be sober, be vigilant; because your adversary the devil, as a roaring lion, walketh about, seeking whom he may devour." In other words, stay woke. We are not just provided the enemy's job description in the book of St. John, but the promise comes when Jesus says, "But I have come that you might have life, and have it more abundantly."

So live and let live. Pursue a life that pleases God the most. Teach your children so they can do the same for the next generation. Observe the positive life cycle and how the positive family legacy will continue.

You would think that the matriarch or patriarch of the family has the most wisdom. Truthfully speaking they have the most experience and at times the most influence. The danger occurs however, when they leverage their wisdom to negatively impact generational growth. Past hurts, unresolved issues, and unforgiveness keeps the family stagnant. Conversely, it's a beautiful picture to see the older generation ushering the new generation into the benefits of forgiveness.

What an incredible opportunity all believers have in being part of the family of God. End time prophecy assures us in St. Luke 12:53 that we will see a day when the family unit breaks down. We are living in that day. The father shall be divided against the son, and the son against the father; the mother against the daughter, and the daughter against the mother; the mother-in-law against her daughter-in-law, and the daughter-in-law against her mother-in-law. But there is hope. The hope lies in the power of forgiveness.

Sometimes, one of the most challenging things for believers—and unbelievers—is to operate in the power of forgiveness.

Maybe you have wondered how many times we should forgive each other. The answer is provided in St. Matthew 18:22. We should forgive each other seventy times seventy, a number that symbolizes boundlessness. Look inwardly. Is the associated stress caused by unforgiveness, resentment, and bitterness worth your time?

Research has taught us that unforgiveness can cause health problems. Hopefully, you will conclude, it's just not worth it. The Bible informs us in St. Matthew 18:34, that if we do not forgive people, we get turned over to the torturers. You do not possess the power needed on your own to forgive. Maybe you tried it, and when you realized you just couldn't do it, you gave up. But with the power of God and, of course, a willingness on your part, you can forgive. If you have ever needed to be forgiven—you must yourself forgive.

Can you imagine being quick to forgive so you can quickly receive the same? Allow me to reiterate, the Bible clearly states that if you want forgiveness, you first have to forgive. But if you don't forgive others, your Father will not forgive your sins.

Keep in mind that one of the things we all have in common is that we all sometimes miss the mark. How many people do you know are exempt from forgiving others? I don't know about you, but I need forgiveness and I also need to forgive on a daily basis. The only person that does not need forgiveness is the person who never makes a mistake.

You probably have heard these two statements made, and maybe have even made them yourself, that *"family is everything* "and *"life is short."* You must forgive quickly because time is not a friend of unforgiveness.

We have a family song. Our sons will always remember the lyrics. Our family's version of the song lyrics goes like this:

Dad: First there's me

MuM: Then there's me

Ryan & Reagan: Then, there's us

All: And that made all of us, we're a family, a family, a family, each like the other

Dad: Father

MuM: Mother

Ryan: Brother

Reagan: Brother

The last line of the song says that the dog came afterward; however, we never had a dog, which is another story. So, as our family expanded to include our first daughter-in-love, we gave her the line, "And then Kiandra came afterward." Now that our youngest son is engaged, we will change the line to include both daughters. The significance surrounding this family song will always be special to our family because we made it our song.

When we took our oldest son to college, we sang our song before the three of us left the University. To my surprise, Ryan didn't seem to mind a bit that we were singing the "family song" in front of his new college roommate. Ryan sang with us because the song meant something to him, as well as to all of us. What does it mean to us? It means we are proud to be a part of God's family, and proud to be a Davis.

Just recently, when Reagan and his fiancé Jessica were leaving our home the day after Christmas, Reagan mentioned the song, but he said, "Let's not sing it until Ryan and Kiandra are here." I thought, *Well, that's something that is really in his heart.* With it in his heart, I can be assured

that the songs, stories, poems, games— I'm so excited—
our children will pass them down to the next generation
and will remember them as heirloom seeds.

Love,
"the MuM"

Self - Exam Questions:

1. What kind of legacy would I like to leave my family?
2. What are some of the steps I can begin to implement right now?
3. Have I anticipated some of the barriers I could encounter in pursuing my family?
4. Am I a team player, or is it all about me?
5. How can I be more supportive of my family members?

Faith Confessions:

I declare by faith Joshua 1:6-9 over my life and the lives of my loved ones. I declare that my family and I are blessed. I will keep this Book of the Law always on my lips; I will meditate on it day and night so that I may be careful to do everything written in it. I realize that the Word of God is providing me with the formula for success. I am further reminded to be strong and courageous, not to be afraid, and not to be discouraged, for the LORD, my God will be with me wherever I go.

"Don't judge each day by the harvest that you reap but by
the seeds that you plant."
-Robert Louis Stevenson

Letter Four

INTO EACH LIFE SOME RAIN MUST FALL

These things I have spoken to you, that in Me you may have peace. In the world you will have tribulation; but be of good cheer, I have overcome the world.
St. John 16:33 NKJV

Dear Beloved,

The old saying is true; into each life, some rain must fall. It's not the type of thing you look forward to, but troubled times will come. No one is exempt from trouble. Trouble cannot be avoided; it cannot be outrun; it cannot be lived above or beneath. What I have learned over the years is that, when troubled times come, you have to deal with it. You may find that it certainly can bring out the best and the worst in you. At any rate, it is essential to remember that it does not last always. Allow me to repeat it. It does not last always.

Imagine if someone said to you, "I have bad news and good news—which do you prefer first?" Studies show that

78% of people would rather hear the bad news first so they can leave a conversation of this type on a good note. Often, you want to get the bad news out of the way, so you say, "Ok, give me the bad news." The bad news is, at different stages of your life, you will experience trouble. After pondering that for a few moments, you then hope for some good news; you're told just to be optimistic. The bottom line is, the Lord has taken care of everything for you. In other words, He has made the crooked ways straight, and He has worked out every detail of your life.

The best advice I could ever give anyone faced with trouble, or problematic issues, is to never run from them. Running from trouble doesn't make it disappear. Instead of running from trouble, face your giants head-on.

Speaking of giants, the Bible records a story about a shepherd boy by the name of David and a giant named Goliath. In the book of 1 Samuel 17, David literally ran right into trouble. Though the two had a physical dispute, David had a brilliant idea. Have you ever had a brilliant idea, one that had victory written all over it? David thought back in his mind and remembered how he had fought lions and bears to protect his father's sheep, and he realized even in the midst of trouble, that God had kept him safe. So, he knew that this God would do the same with his match with Goliath. David defeated Goliath with five smooth stones and a sling.

David used the power of the tongue when he declared to Goliath, "You come against me with sword, spear, and javelin, but I come against you in the name of the Lord Almighty, the God of the armies of Israel, whom you have defied." David's faith assured him that the Lord would deliver Goliath into his hand. And that's just the way the story ends. The giant was defeated. When your faith rises to the occasion, keep in mind that your giants are defeated as well. The moral of the story is to use what the Lord has given you to get what He has promised.

If you have enough faith to believe that the Lord could use you to defeat your enemies, accept that you will survive any trial. The fantastic news in St. John 16:33 is—though trials and tribulations are usually categorized as bad news—Jesus didn't leave us hopeless. He added a very significant encouraging phrase when He said these five words, "But be of good cheer." The most important thing to know is that He has overcome the world. An overcomer is one who triumphs over an obstacle. Indeed, this is good news for the believer.

According to the Word of God, there are ways to thrive in difficult times. When we find ourselves becoming overly anxious about life's issues, the human part of us wonders just how in the world will we get out of certain situations. Whether it is problems in our families, homes, churches, jobs, communities, or schools, we can undoubtedly take the Apostle Paul's advice. In the following passage, he advises us to pray and cease worrying. That is when real peace comes. Philippians 4:6-7 (NKJV) tells us, "Be anxious for nothing, but in everything by prayer and supplication, with thanksgiving, let your requests be made known to God; and the peace of God, which surpasses all understanding, will guard your hearts and minds through Christ Jesus."

The Bible gives you peace as the prophet Isaiah delivers a message from God as recorded in Isaiah 41:10 that simply says, "Fear thou not; for I am with thee: be not dismayed; for I am thy God: I will strengthen thee; yea, I will help thee; yea, I will uphold thee with the right hand of my righteousness."

Our human response again is to wonder, how can we not be fearful. Maybe you think that you don't know what the next day holds in your life, not even the next second; well, you never did. I don't remember a time in my life when the Lord was not right there helping me by providing me all the tools needed—His love, wisdom, strength, provision, and peace.

Life has its own set of disappointments. Some things happen unexpectedly, and sometimes you will go through storms in your life. There is one thing that I have found out about storms. No matter if it's a natural storm or a spiritual one, whatever damage is done, God is a restorer.

Have you noticed it's when you're in a storm that it seems as if you're never coming out? It may also appear as if you are the only one going through the storm. These statements are not valid. Have you thought about who dictates when you're coming out of a storm? It's much more than a cliché when we say God takes us through to bring us out. Have you ever wondered what life would be like if there were no troubles, no disappointments, no tribulations, no trials, and no storms?

If I were writing a course entitled "Earthly Living 101," I would have to include in the syllabus that very shortly after birth, or even during the process of being born, trouble will rear its ugly head. I was just thinking recently that if you don't want to get hurt, don't come out of the birth canal. At that point, you don't have a choice. I get that. Just to be clear, life comes with pain. The Apostle Paul talks about it in 2 Corinthians 4:7–18:

> But we have this treasure in earthen vessels, that the excellency of the power may be of God, and not of us.
>
> We are troubled on every side, yet not distressed; we are perplexed, but not in despair; Persecuted, but not forsaken; cast down, but not destroyed; Always bearing about in the body the dying of the Lord Jesus, that the life also of Jesus might be made manifest in our body.
>
> For we which live are always delivered unto death for Jesus' sake, that the life also of Jesus might be made manifest in our mortal flesh.
>
> So, then death worketh in us, but life in you. We having the same spirit of faith, according as it is written, I

believed, and therefore have I spoken; we also believe, and therefore speak;

Knowing that He which raised up the Lord Jesus shall raise up us also by Jesus, and shall present us with you. For all things are for your sakes, that the abundant grace might through the thanksgiving of many redound to the glory of God.

For which because we faint not; but though our outward man perishes, yet the inward man is renewed day by day. For our light affliction, which is but for a moment, worketh for us a far more exceeding and eternal weight of glory;

While we look not at the things which are seen, but at the things which are not seen: for the things which are seen are temporal; but the things which are not seen are eternal.

If it were not for the mercy of God, there would be no hope for any of us. Suffering and tribulations are common experiences in every life but hold on to your advantage. I call it the believer's advantage, which reminds us we can depend on God. The believer's advantage lets us know that, as a child of God, we have been provided certain rights and privileges that "outsiders of the ark of safety" cannot enjoy. Always remember that God is a faithful God. Lamentations 3:22-23 bears that out:

It is of the LORD's mercies that we are not consumed, because His compassions fail not. They are new every morning: great is thy faithfulness.

Another scripture that provides hope in difficult times is 1 Peter 5:7 (NIV) it says, "Cast all your anxiety on him because he cares for you."

Some would say this is easier said than done. But when you are in a relationship with someone, there is a certain amount of trust you have in that person. The Bible states that if you have mustard seed faith, you can speak to the mountain, and nothing shall be impossible for you, according to St. Matthew 17:20.

The Bible also encourages you to build your hope when you meditate on scriptures like these:

For I reckon that the sufferings of this present time are not worthy to be compared with the glory which shall be revealed in us.
- Romans 8:18

I can do all things through him who strengthens me.
- Philippians 4:13

For I know the thoughts that I think toward you, saith the LORD, thoughts of peace, and not of evil, to give you an expected end.
- Jeremiah 29:11

My brethren, count it all joy when ye fall into divers temptations; Knowing this, that the trying of your faith worketh patience. But let patience have her perfect work, that ye may be perfect and entire, wanting nothing.
- James 1:2-4

The LORD also will be a refuge for the oppressed, a refuge in times of trouble.
And they that know thy name will put their trust in thee: for thou, LORD, hast not forsaken them that seek thee.
- Psalm 9:9-10

The Word of God signals a warning in Job 14:1, it reminds us that, "Man that is born of a woman is of few days and full of trouble." Romans 5:3 lets us know, "And not only so, but we glory in tribulations also: knowing that tribulation worketh patience."

So, there is a purpose for the pain. I am happy the Word of God didn't say, "thinking" or "hoping" or "wishing" that tribulation works for us, but the Bible distinctly says "knowing" tribulation works patience. As long as it's working something for my good, I don't always have to understand, but my acceptance is far better.

Trouble has a purpose. It's not about the trouble as much as it is about how you handle the difficult situations— the things that bother, bind, and hinder you. I am talking about the difficulties, predicaments, plights, problems, fears, worries, concerns, inconveniences, nuisances, disturbances, calamities, catastrophes, crises, negativities, delays, disputes, afflictions, intrusions, irritations, trials, pain, and ordeals.

Have you noticed that everyone handles trouble differently? We are all at times prone to carry a level of doubt, even as we profess to walk by faith and trust in God. It's like being in a battle of two wars— internal and external raging at the same time. While there are all kinds of temporary fixes and remedies to calm you down, but in reality, they may shut you down. God is always there to help you.

Imagine life as a classroom, and every day is a test. Much of the trouble you face is only a test. You must remember that God did not set up the test to fail you, but He set up the test to advance you.

Such was the case of Abraham sacrificing his son, Isaac. The story is recounted in Genesis 22. Abraham was willing to sacrifice Isaac. Ultimately God did not require a human sacrifice, but He accepted Abraham's willingness to offer his son. God is always calling upon us to make decisions that seem to shatter the fulfillment of His promises. Yet here is where faith is essential. Exercising your faith will give you the first glimpse of victory.

Can you just imagine Abraham and Isaac walking alone up the mountain? Abraham could have thought that this was the end of the promise. However, every step he took was in faith. Somehow, he had to have known God would not let him down. Thus, Abraham advanced to the faith hall of fame.

The Bible also records another very familiar story of a man named Job. Reading his story will reveal to you how trouble meets triumph. Job was a wealthy and upright man, and when trouble came into his life, he lost his worldly possessions, including his children, and his health. If you have lived long enough, one of the things you appreciate and don't take for granted is your good health. It is safe to say that Job had entered a season in his life that was full of suffering and trouble. He was also in a season that required him to make a command decision. The decision to silence the noise of outside distractions, and to increase his focus and trust in God. The caption over Job's life should read: "The enemy could not touch him without God's consent." And that's the same message over your life as well.

Job's friends naturally but incorrectly assessed that Job's troubles resulted from sin in his life. Though Job was a righteous man, it did not exempt him from trouble in the same way that it does not exempt you from trouble. Job's wife couldn't understand the trial, but she could not convince him to give up on God.

There are lessons to be learned while suffering. Keep in mind that there is a purpose for this, and there will be glory in your story. The objective is always to demonstrate the sovereignty of God, His grace, and His truth.

Job's faithfulness prevailed. As Job laments in his closing remarks, all that he had gone through left him with feelings of not being treated fairly and a lot of emotions. You may have heard it said, and, indeed, Satan doesn't know everything. If Satan had known that Job would be blessed two-fold in the end, do you think he would have suggested Job's name in the first place?

One of my most significant takeaways (as one of our

Elders so profoundly expounded, at one of our Wednesday Night Bible Studies) is, "the devil works for God." Again, he could not touch Job without the Lord's consent.

But through it all, you need to examine trouble when it comes and know that the Lord will strengthen you and your experience. And your testimony, when shared, will help others. The most important thing to remember is that "the glory" goes to God.

Rain is most associated with sadness, rejection, or despair, but who says it must be this way? Rain isn't always bad. Spiritually speaking, rain represents rebirth.

After the rain, there is a rainbow.

Love,
"the MuM"

Self - Exam Questions:

1. Based on my relationship with the Lord, how do I think I will handle trouble the next time my name is mentioned before the Lord?
2. How did I handle my last trouble season?
3. How could I have handled it better?
4. Can my faithfulness prevail as Job's did?
5. Was there help available for me when I was seemingly down and out?
6. What advice can I share with someone else who is going through the worst of times?

Faith Confessions

I declare, by faith, I am a world overcomer. In this life, there will be troubled times, but the Bible lets me know that the Lord has overcome the world. I declare and believe by faith that God is our refuge and strength, an ever-present help in trouble. I declare and believe by faith that the name of the Lord is a strong tower; the righteous run into it and are safe. I declare and believe by faith that the joy of the Lord is my strength. I declare and believe by faith that the Lord's plans are to prosper me, not harm me; they are plans to give me hope and a future.

"If you suffer, thank God! It is a sure sign that you are alive."
-Elbert Hubbard

Letter Five

BE YOURSELF

I will praise You, for I am fearfully and wonderfully made;
Marvelous are Your works,
And that my soul knows very well.
Psalm 139:14 NKJV

Dear Beloved,

Know that there is no other person in the world that can be a better you than you. I discovered two important truths about the uniqueness in me, and I offer them for your consideration to help you embrace your identity. Truthfully, I must accept that I am unique, and I respect the uniqueness of others.

One of my greatest pet peeves is when someone asks my opinion, and when it is given, discredits me because I disagree with their beliefs. Can I be me? Can you accept me to be who I am and stand in my truths? Likewise, can I allow you to be who you are, and stand in your truths?

In an orchestra, there are a diversity of instruments each capable of producing a distinct sound. It's up to the musicians to yield their skills under the hand of a master conductor, who produces a pleasing sound to the listeners. The unity of the instruments is priceless. They blend in perfect harmony. The conductor directs, unifies, and sets the tempo; however, the musicians play their parts to bring the most pleasing results to the ear. Each one is unique; each one has a part, and each one is being counted on to bring a special flavor to the performance.

In the orchestra, the violin will not sound like the cello, and the flute will not sound like the oboe or the tuba. But when teamwork is demonstrated, all of the instruments provide an inspiring experience that encourages audiences to enjoy the arts.

We are just as unique as the instruments in an orchestra; however, we make the sad mistake of comparing ourselves to others, which I consider terrible judgment. When you compare yourself with others, you are telling God that, instead of making you unique, you wish He had made you like everyone else.

There is a virtual community network called social media, which is an extraordinary tool used for everything from building your personal brand to finding lost family members and friends. When used correctly, it is a powerful tool; however, you need to gain control over it. Why? Because this same network can cause many distractions. It can place you in an awkward situation where you are always trying to measure up to or surpass others. How can you truly enjoy your life when you're always trying to imitate someone else? You can learn a lot from others, but you should always embrace the person you greet in the mirror.

The person in the mirror can always use improvements; however, when was the last time you appreciated this person? There is a time and a season for everything. You don't share the same season as your next-door neighbor or your work team member. It is essential to know just who you are and what season you are experiencing in life, so be careful not to compare yourself with anyone else and what's going on in their season.

In any relationship, it is always important to remember the golden rule, which simply states to treat others as you want to be treated. If you know who you are, you already know you want to be treated with dignity and respect; all it takes is remembering to do likewise to others. It is also important to respect everyone and their uniqueness. Relationships are always better when people try to get along.

Understanding yourself is also vital. How many times have you heard it said, "I know me?" You may be one of the ones trying to figure out that person in the mirror. But how can you and I work well together when I do not know who you are, and admittedly, you do not know who I am either?

The Bible encourages us in Romans 12:16 (NIV) to, "Live in harmony with one another. Do not be proud but be willing to associate with people of low position. Do not be conceited." Being you that God created you to be, should be something you aspire to do. It is a compliment to God that He made you unique and fully equipped to accomplish your destination with His help. Second Peter 1:3 bears that out:

According as his divine power hath given unto us all things that pertain unto life and godliness, through the knowledge of Him that hath called us to glory and virtue.

Let's reflect on the scripture from Genesis 1:27 the Word informs us:

So God created man in His own image, in the image of God He created him; male and female He created them.

We live in a world of images. Many of these images are displayed daily on all social media platforms, on television, mobile devices, and even in your head, but have you ever pondered what God's image is all about? Let's break it down.

An image is a representation of the external form of a person or thing. According to Genesis 1:26, on the final day of creation, after making man in His image, and giving him dominion over fish, birds, cattle, and everything that creeps on the earth, God completed His work with an "exceptional customized touch. "And the LORD God formed man of the dust of the ground and breathed into his nostrils the breath of life, and man became a living soul. Humankind possesses body, soul, and spirit, and is made to resemble God. In other words, God is saying you are fearfully and wonderfully made in my image. Humans are set apart from the animal world. God intended for you to walk in your God-given authority on earth, and you have the ability to commune with Him. Aren't you happy to be on that side of the spectrum—a part of the human world—with the advantages of having body, mind, and soul?

The context of Psalm 139:14 is absolutely the incredible nature of our physical bodies. Why do you think the human body is the most complex and unique organism in the world? The uniqueness that all people possess speaks volumes about the mind of our Father.

Truly know you are fearfully and wonderfully made, down to the tiniest cell in your body. We were made from love, and we were made to love. Some of the most exciting things God did for you are:

1. He carefully shaped and knitted you together in your mother's womb with tender loving care.

2. God custom-made the blueprint for your life. You are unique. No, you didn't just evolve into who you are today; instead, because you were on the mind of God, you were created and designed with a divine

purpose.

3. The research shows that the 2018 world population was over 7 billion people, with one being born every 7 seconds. But guess what? There is no one on the planet like you. Every individual's DNA, for all practical purposes, is unique.

Now that alone should bump up your praise!!!!!

Ephesians 2:10 informs us, "For we are his workmanship, created in Christ Jesus unto good works, which God hath before ordained that we should walk in them." God has provided skills and artistry to accomplish every mission assigned to you, which also allows you to be you.

Sometimes you don't allow others to get to know the real "you" for many reasons. One reason may be that if others got to know the real you, they would not like you, and no one wants to be rejected. Keep in mind that your uniqueness is what sets you apart and makes you different.

One of the first attacks of the enemy is to attack your identity. If he can keep you from knowing who you are, half of his battle is won. However, when you understand who you are and whose you are, it should lead you to utilize what I refer to as "your best self-investment strategies." I am not talking about growth stocks, momentum investing, or fundamental analysis; instead, how about investing in yourself, investing in others, and investing in the kingdom of God? Listed below are some of the best investment strategies for you to consider.

Investing in You:

Read more books. Books will take you places that you never expected to go. Studies show that reading reduces stress as well as helps you to concentrate and focus. There is undoubtedly a sense of empowerment gained when reading is one of your hobbies.

Expand your territory. Do something you have never done before. Surprise yourself. Increase your skills and abilities by trying something you have always wanted to do.

Never stop learning. There is always something new to learn. When you remain a student in life, you will be relevant and innovative, and young people get a kick out of seeing their elders as relatable people.

Investing in Others:

Be a good listener. Most people would agree that it's more challenging to listen than to speak. But try it. Just because you know some things does not mean you always have to talk. Train yourself to listen and try not to focus your thoughts on the next thing you want to communicate and miss what is being said to you.

Become a mentor. I believe that your purpose on earth is not just to live for yourself; it has to be to serve others. Be a giver of your time; take someone under your wings and guide them.

Sow into others. You may have heard it said what you make happen for others; God will make happen for you.

Investing in the Kingdom:

Be a tither. In other words, be obedient to the Word of God. My revelation on tithing is this; if you don't pay your rent or mortgage, you will eventually be evicted. The same thing happened in the book of Genesis when Adam and Eve touched the forbidden fruit, which represented the tithe (I thank my Bishop for that revelation); however, they were evicted from their beautiful garden home. Don't touch God's tithe. It's not worth the trouble.

Be generous. Do something for someone who can't pay you back. If you are a helper and possess a giving, generous heart, you absolutely cannot lose. You will always prosper. God's Word backs this up in St. Luke 6:35.

Be a good steward. Use your gifts and talents to bless others. You can use them to reach the lost. Being a good steward is important to God and should be your priority as well. When you do this, you honor Him as we bless others.

Love,
"the MuM"

Self - Exam Questions:

1. Why do I sometimes think I want to be someone other than myself?
2. What is it that attracts me to someone else's life?
3. How confident do I feel being me?
4. How confident am I with embracing me?
5. Do I embrace the uniqueness of others?

Faith Confessions

I am made in God's image. The proof is in Genesis 1:26-27. God has blessed me to be a blessing to others. I am fearfully and wonderfully made. The evidence is in Psalm 139:14. I praise God for the variety of people He created, but I will not forget to praise Him for how He made me. I am made the righteousness of God in Christ Jesus. The evidence is in 2 Corinthians 5:20-21. I am an ambassador for Christ. I am a God pleaser. The Holy Spirit gives me the power to reflect the righteousness of God.

"To avoid criticism, do nothing, say nothing, and be nothing."
-Elbert Hubbard

Letter Six

LIVING ON THE POSITIVE SIDE OF LIFE

Finally, brothers and sisters, whatever is true, whatever is noble, whatever is right, whatever is pure, whatever is lovely, whatever is admirable—if anything is excellent or praiseworthy—think about such things.
Philippians 4:8 NIV

Dear Beloved,

Just in case you haven't noticed, it's not the easiest thing to maintain a positive mind and attitude. Before you know it, you get in a conversation with someone who's whining and complaining, and if you're not extra careful, you will jump right on the bandwagon, though it may not be your intention.

I believe positive thinking begins with what's in your heart, because out of your heart spring the issues of life according to Proverbs 4:23 (NKJV). It starts with what you have been taught, either by a parent, teacher, or guardian. It takes focus and willingness to desire to live on the positive side of life.

However, it doesn't mean you can or even should ignore what's going on in the world. The question is, how can you live on the positive side of life when so many negative and ungodly things are taking place?

Let's examine that place of positiveness. What's on your mind right now? No matter what is going on in your life, you have the ability and the option to be positive or to be negative. It is a matter of choice; your thoughts lead to your actions. Being adamant about having a positive attitude will allow you to be a positive thinker and speaker, resulting in your efforts being positive deeds. You may, at times, feel like you're the minority, but keep on planting positive seeds, and your harvest will be extraordinary.

We are living in a very health-conscious society, with a focus on nutrition and exercise. Equally crucial to humankind is healthy thought choices. Contrary to what you may have heard, you can control your thoughts. You cannot prevent them from popping up in your mind; however, you can control what happens to them after they have made their entry. Making sure you are living to please God is a great goal, but how are you going to accomplish this mission with ugly, stinking thinking?

The Word of God in Proverbs 23:7a (NKJV) lets us know, "For as he thinks in his heart, so is he." The most anointed person you know has ugly thoughts at times. The most important thing to remember about evil thoughts is not to allow them to get out of control. Have a plan for ugly thoughts. Reach deep within yourself to replace a negative thought with something positive.

You can execute a map designed for evil thoughts before you have one. Let's be clear; it doesn't matter how saved you are; negative thoughts are going to visit. You are the only one that can determine how long they stay.

The very next time you have a terrible thought, my

recommendation is to fill your mind with God's truths. You might not be able to open your Bible at the time, but during your reading and meditating, memorize scripture as much as possible to be used at the most needed time.

Consider using this formula: Reading and meditating on God's Word + keeping your environment toxic free = positive energy. Begin with the first variable, reading and meditating on God's Word. God's Word is 100% positive, and it is true. If you read it from a version that you can understand, you will be amazingly surprised by the helpful information that awaits you. It's very similar to a term we have used for years to highlight our youths' reading skills. Like children "hooked on phonics," you will be hooked on God's Word and perhaps become more excited about following His ways.

Sports, television, comedians, and the Internet can entertain you. Still, God's Word was not designed to entertain but ultimately to educate you and propel you to a victorious, changed life.

Let's look at the second variable in the equation. It is keeping your environment (your space) from toxic people. It certainly does not mean to live as a hermit, though the thought may come to mind. But that's just not possible. It wouldn't work anyway because God created you for fellowship. People, along with positive and negative situations, are what we have to deal with in life. Let's face it, living on the positive side of life has its benefits while living on the negative side of life has its repercussions.

Creating a positive space involves making it a known fact that you will not allow the negativity of others to spill over and affect you. It also has to be known that you will not tolerate gossip, and you will not entertain strife. It's just not who you aspire to be. Create a space that lets others know that you're not going to be treated like a garbage disposal. People have to know you don't roll like that.

Being a positive thinker does not mean you bury your

head in the sand and pretend the world is not continually infiltrating your thought life with negativity. You cannot ignore the constant breaking news on your mobile devices, your television, and your radios. Unpleasant situations are happening every second. Being a positive thinker means taking control over the low hanging fruit and reaching for higher heights. The Psalmist declares in Psalm 94:19 (NLT) "When doubts filled my mind, your comfort gave me renewed hope and cheer." Thus, your positive energy is experienced. When others enter into your presence, they can tell right away that you're different on purpose.

How can you keep your mind on the best when you keep hearing the worst? You have to be deliberate in choosing your environment. What you hear has a significant impact on you. Just as faith comes by hearing and hearing by the Word of God, fear and doubt come by hearing a false report.

Let's look at an example of keeping it positive after you have just experienced a hostile situation. If you decide to share your situation, stay out of the details. Do not allow the negativity of others to shut you down. Have you noticed that positive thinking people can find pleasantness in the most horrendous situations? My thoughts are that negative thinking people will find fault with heaven; if that was a possibility.

How one person views the world is a matter of personal perspective. There are no two people that will view circumstances the same way.

The Bible records a situation found in the book of Numbers, chapters 13 and 14. Caleb was one of the spies sent by Moses to scout out the land of Canaan. The people of the land were advised by these two courageous leaders to proceed immediately to take the land. One spy was sent from each tribe, but they were not the ones appointed as census takers. Interestingly enough, they were not sent to fight any battles but merely to bring back a report about the land. Their forty-day trip over the entire land convinced them that the land was desirable, but 10 of the 12 saw the glass as half empty because they felt the land couldn't be conquered.

Put yourself in the spy's place; are you quick to overthink a situation? Are you quick to see the worst of a situation? Are you quick to avoid taking a risk? Are you fearful about how you measure up compared to others?

Joshua and Caleb's report was declined. However, it was a favorable recommendation, the one which should have spurred the people to action because of their faith in God. There seemed no doubt it was the descendants of Anak, the legendary giants who frightened the spies and even filled them with terror. Despite the pleas of Joshua and Caleb, the people refused to have faith. Maybe they were not aware that the Christian life is a faith walk from start to finish. The people had the audacity to murmur against Moses and Aaron.

Hear ye, hear ye, please do not put your mouth on your spiritual leaders. The only thing that should proceed out of your mouth is a prayer to the Lord because complaining about God's leaders will lead to your detriment. Keep in mind that they are accountable to Him and Him only.

God was not pleased, and He threatened to disinherit the people and make Moses' family a great nation and replace them. Moses did what great spiritual leaders do today; he interceded for the same people complaining about him and his brother. God changed his mind—He reconsidered, but the penalty was stern. The penalty included that no man over twenty years of age would be allowed to enter the Promised Land except the two spies who brought favorable recommendations. Alarmed by God's decrees, the people then attempted to enter the land but were met with disaster. God was not with them. That's one place you do not want to be—where the blessings are not.

Will you be as fierce as Caleb to take on what appears to

be more than you can handle? Will you trust God to bring you through? Or will you keep wandering in wilderness experiences, making no progress at all because of the spirit of fear combined with a false perception?

We have often asked the question, is the glass half empty or is the glass half full? It was thought that a positive thinking person would answer, "The glass is half full," and every negative thinking person would answer, "The glass is half empty." But would you consider a glass that needs refilling?

There comes a time when you have to make a determination, to answer this question, "Whose report am I going to believe?"

Love,
"the MuM"

Self - Exam Questions:

1. Which question best describes my outlook in life: am I ready for the world, or is the world ready for me?
2. Do I make a point of seeing the good in situations and people, or am I always seeing the negatives?
3. Do I allow the naysayers to influence my true feelings?
4. How can I spread positivity?

Faith Confessions:

I decree and declare, according to 1 Corinthians 2:16 and Philippians 2:5, I have the Jesus kind of mind. I decree and declare, according to Romans 12:2, I am reminded not to be conformed to this world, but to be transformed by the renewing of my mind, that I may prove what is that good, and acceptable, and perfect, will of God. I have a made-up mind to choose the positive side of life. I decree and declare, according to Isaiah 26:3, the Lord will keep me in perfect peace if I keep my mind on Him.

"Positive anything is better than negative nothing."
-Elbert Hubbard

Letter Seven

YOUR GIFTS TALENTS AND ABILITIES

As each one has received a gift, minister it to one another, as good stewards of the manifold grace of God. If anyone speaks, let him speak as the oracles of God. If anyone ministers, let him do it as with the ability which God supplies, that in all things God may be glorified through Jesus Christ, to whom belong the glory and the dominion forever and ever.
1 Peter 4:10-11 NKJV

Dear Beloved,

What motivates you? Without giving it too much thought, what makes you feel the most fulfilled? Perhaps you have heard that the world doesn't move to the beat of just one drum, meaning everyone is not motivated in the same ways, which is a beautiful thing. The kingdom of God is diversified. Hallelujah.

Spoiler Alert: Every one of us has received a gift to minister to one another. With whose ability are we to operate? God is the supplier. He created everyone with unique abilities and talents to serve.

Sometimes we're not even aware of the giftings that God gives us. Often it takes another individual to help pull them out of us. Or other times, we take our gifts, talents, and abilities (I like to call them GTAs) for granted, as if they are so insignificant. But remember, the gift-giver gives them freely, and He gives them to whom He can trust.

You need to pause and give God thanks for all He has given you. Your talents can be your unique personality, and no character is exactly like yours. It could be your ability to provide kind words— we truly need more of that. Maybe you have musical abilities or a strong determination to live an abundant life. It could also be giving, preaching, wisdom, compassion, teaching skills, charisma, communication, or other skills the people of God so desperately need. We need to be wise and put our GTAs to good use and help others.

We are all part of the Body of Christ. Just think—one big family with God as our Father. Don't you think it's about time to stop letting God's gifts collect dust? You either use your gifts, or they will be wasted away, and if that's the case, someone is missing out on something unique and wonderful—your gifts. God has given them to you for a purpose. My question is, how are you using your GTAs to edify people and to glorify Him?

Maybe you have asked the questions, what are my gifts, and what am I anointed to do? Recently in one of my text messages to my son Ryan, I asked him, "Are you working today?" and his answer to me was, "No, ma'am, I am operating in my anointing today." That answer was impressive and given as a result of being raised in a teaching ministry—a place where he took great notes and put them into action.

It makes a parent more than proud to see our children operate in their unique giftings. Ryan and Reagan have the gift of teaching, among other gifts. With the anointing of the Lord on them, they are vessels used unto honor. And that will be the same for you, and the young people in your life. Ask God to anoint your gift and use it for His glory.

The word "anoint" means to smear or rub with oil, to consecrate for office, typically as part of a religious ceremony. Acts 10:38 informs us, "How God anointed Jesus of Nazareth with the Holy Spirit and power: who went about doing good, and healing all that were oppressed of the devil, for God was with Him."

The Word of God informs us that these gifts are provided to each of us so we can help each other. Just imagine, if everyone recognized their spiritual gifts, and used them, everyone in the Body of Christ would benefit.

God is the gift-giver, and no, we don't get to choose our gifts; however, we need to accept our gifts and execute as the Spirit directs us. When you think about it, our gifts fit our personalities, and who knows us better than the gift-giver? He knows exactly who He can trust with these beautiful effective gifts.

Romans 12:6-8 (NLT) lets us know that, "In His grace, God has given us different gifts for doing certain things well. So, if God has given you the ability to prophesy, speak out with as much faith as God has given you. If your gift is serving others, serve them well. If you are a teacher, teach well. If your gift is to encourage others, be encouraging. If it is giving, give generously. If God has given you leadership abilities, take the responsibility seriously. And if you have a gift for showing kindness to others, do it gladly."

First Peter 4:10-11 lets us know something exciting about all of us. Again, our gifts were designed to serve each other. The Bible also encourages us that if you serve, remember to do it with God's strength. By doing so, God will be praised through Jesus Christ, and the power and glory belong to Him forever.

Other scriptures to help you understand your giftings:

Not slothful in business; fervent in spirit; serving the Lord;
- Romans 12:11

For who do you know that really knows you, knows your heart? And even if they did, is there anything they would discover in you that you could take credit for? Isn't everything you have and everything you are sheer gifts from God? So what's the point of all this comparing and competing? You already have all you need. You already have more access to God than you can handle. Without bringing either Apollos or me into it, you're sitting on top of the world—at least God's world—and we're right there, sitting alongside you!
- 1 Corinthians 4:7-8, TM

But he giveth more grace. Wherefore he saith, God resisted the proud, but giveth grace unto the humble.
- James 4:6

And let us consider one another to provoke unto love and to good works.
- Hebrews 10:24

But exhort one another daily, while it is called Today; lest any of you be hardened through the deceitfulness of sin.
- Hebrews 3:13, NKJV

For as we have many members in one body, and all members have not the same office.
So we, being many, are one body in Christ, and every one members one of another."
- Romans 12:4-5

For as the body is one, and hath many members, and all the members of that one body, being many, are one body: so also is Christ.
-1 Corinthians 12:12

Now ye are the body of Christ, and members in particular.
-1 Corinthians 12:27

There is a story found in St. Matthew 25:14-30 about a man going on a trip who called his servants and turned his money (talents) over to them. To one man, he gave five talents, to another two, and to another one, based on their ability. Then he went on his trip. The one who received five talents went out at once and invested them and earned five more. In the same way, the one who had two talents gained two more. But the one who received one talent went off, dug a hole in the ground, and buried his master's money. After a long time, the master of those servants returned and settled accounts with them. The one who had received five talents came up and brought five more talents. Master, he said, you gave me five talents. See, I've earned five more talents. His master told him, Well done, good and trustworthy servant! Since you've been trustworthy with a small amount, I'll put you in charge of a large amount. Come and share your master's joy!

The moral of this story is if you invest well, you will receive a grand return on your investment. If God can trust you with little, He has no issues trusting you when little becomes much. God wants us to use what He provides to bring Him glory. The good news is everyone on earth has GTAs. Many people tend to downplay their GTAs. The critical thing to remember is to be grateful and gracious with the GTAs you have been provided.

A spiritual gift is an endowment or extraordinary power given by the Holy Spirit. Talent is the ability to do easily what others find hard to do. Ability is the possession of the means or skill to do something. The GTAs are designed so that we all get blessed.

There are so many ways we can serve and minister to each other. Some people are just naturally talented. Others have exceptional skills in coaching, leadership, problem-solving, time management, customer service, and computer skills, to name only a few.

Along with being a good steward, we have a responsibility not only to society but, most importantly, to the gift-giver to use our gifts. If not correctly used, the person or persons to be inspired by your gifts will miss an important date with destiny.

Do you wake up in the mornings wondering who could be positively impacted by what you have? How's that for adding purpose to your life? One of our problems is that instead of realizing our gifts as special and unique, we try to imitate someone else because we like the way they speak, lead, teach or preach. In essence we like the way they glorify God. There's nothing wrong with admiring others gifts; however, it is essential to desire to be the you that God made.

While traveling through Lumberton North Carolina a few years ago, we stopped at a Chick-fil-A. The sign on the door read, "We need your talents—Apply inside." I remember thinking about how we live in a team-oriented culture. The key is for people to work together towards a common objective.

However, if every member of the team had the same talent, the same ability, or the same gifts, how effective do you think the team would be? How effective would we be if everyone were the same or everyone had only one thing to offer the world, instead of the diversity that was meant from the very beginning?

Your greatest gift to the world is love. In my opinion, love has always been the main ingredient; however, it is in such short supply. Remember, love is an action word. The

Bible clearly defines love in St. John 3:16. Our heavenly Father loved us so much that He did something for us. He placed all of His love in action when He gave His only begotten son, Jesus. He gave us Himself. That's love.

Love,
"the MuM"

Self - Exam Questions:

1. (If unknown) How can I find out what my spiritual gifts are to the Body of Christ?
2. (If known) What do I consider to be my primary gift?
3. What are some of the activities I can engage in to connect with my giftings?

Faith Confessions

Thank you, Father God, that your Spirit hands out a variety of lovely gifts. Thank you, Father God, for entrusting me with your spiritual gifts. Use me as a vessel of your power to edify the body of Christ. Thank You Father God, for wisdom and discernment to fulfill your purpose and plan in my life. Make serving your people my number one priority, in Jesus' name. Help me to use my gifts, talents, abilities, and skills to bless your people and to glorify your name.

"A great man does not seek applause or place; he seeks for truth; he seeks the road to happiness, and what he ascertains, he gives to others."
-Robert Green Ingersoll

Letter Eight

PURPOSE

*I cry out to God Most High, to God, who will fulfill his
purpose for me.*
Psalm 57:2 NLT

Dear Beloved,

Were you aware that everyone on earth was brought
here for a divine purpose? God thought up every one of
us; however, God had a reason for thinking us up. For the
newborn that didn't live a full 24 hours of life, though, it's
complicated to understand why God nevertheless had a
purpose for that child. There are many books and articles
written on this subject, but for believers, it is vital to take
an in-depth look into the purpose of purpose in our lives.
Purpose is the reason why something is done or used; it is
the aim of or intention of something.

God had a purpose when He created the universe. God
did absolutely nothing without purpose. To understand
God's purpose, we must go back to the book of beginnings,

the book of Genesis. We must realize that we are a unique creation. When God created plant and animal life, He said that each one was made according to their kind, but for humankind, He made us in His image. Isn't that special? He had a purpose for doing so. Genesis 1:27-28 further informs us that God blessed them, meaning humankind, and God's mandate to us is to prosper, reproduce, fill the earth, and undoubtedly take charge.

As mentioned in a previous letter, God gave humankind dominion and responsibility for the fish in the sea and birds in the air, and for everything that moves on the face of the earth. God has a purpose for the moon, sun, stars, trees, flowers, sunshine, rain, and the snow. But the remarkable fact is, God is sovereign, and He orders everything according to His desire.

Many of us have questions about our purpose. It doesn't matter your age or stage. If you are not sure where your true purpose lies, stay encouraged. Many people have not been able to pinpoint God's purpose for their lives, so they end up sitting on the sidelines of life, watching others play, and win.

The questions regarding purpose never seem to cease. They are questions such as who am I? Where do I belong? Why am I here? And who am I here to help? If you are one of those people who ever wondered about God's purpose for your life, again, I offer you Romans 8:28, which says, "And we know that all things work together for good to them that love God, to them who are the called according to his purpose." This passage is probably one of the most memorized and quoted verses in the New Testament. This Scripture brings so much comfort, direction, and hope to believers every time it's read.

What we have to know based on the Word of God is that all things are not-so-good, but all things work for the good. We sometimes wonder how that works. For you, it depends on how much you trust God. Remember, He's the worker. In life, all of us experience good times, and we sometimes experience not- so-good times. But if we allow God to work His master plan based on His blueprint and purpose for our lives, He will ultimately use those not-so-good experiences to bring out the best for each one of us.

God will work something so amazing in your life that it will result in a testimony you will not be able to keep to yourself. Again, you will find that coming out of your trial will allow you to minister to someone when they are going through troubling times.

Have you ever considered some of the things you have gone through in your life that just had to happen? There was just no way around it. I was talking to my husband just recently, and we reached a conclusion—and perhaps you'll agree—that the older you get, the more you reflect on your life, and sometimes you can figure out why things happened the way they did. A greater purpose was on God's mind. Some things had to happen just because they were a part of God's plan.

Jesus' purpose is explained to us in God's Word. When we understand His purpose, we can rejoice with every trial He encountered, every miracle He performed, and every lesson He taught. In St. Mark 8:31 Jesus taught His disciples a few things about His purpose. He let them know that He would suffer, and He would be rejected. The lesson Jesus taught was that He would be put to death. But His purpose would be fully fulfilled and come alive three days later when He conquered death, hell, and the grave. His purpose brought life to us all.

This passage undoubtedly lets us know it took death to bring life. I am reminded of a very memorable experience that took place in our family. On March 1, 1989, my grandmother received her wings. My sister Tan was nine months pregnant, and what felt like such a sobering time for all of us turned into pure joy in the very early morning. So real are the words from Psalm 30:5, where it reminds us that weeping may endure for a night, but joy comes in the morning. My grandmother's homegoing service was held on March 5, and later that evening, my sister went into labor.

One thing for sure, a lot of the family members were there for the birth of my niece that would not have been in town if it had not been for my grandmother's death. But we were all there, and the new life was so refreshing and highly encouraging. It was like God was saying, "I got y'all." Very early the next morning of March 6, we were met with a brand-new life. God turned our mourning into dancing. I was in my 20s, and that may have been the first time I remember feeling and knowing I was in the hollow of His hands. My testimony at that point was God moves through all kinds of situations to fulfill His purpose.

When I think about purpose, I am quickly reminded that God places people on earth to fulfill their ambitions for certain times in history. As mentioned in a previous letter, when we fully understand that God works in seasons, we need to know our season. We can then know that our purpose here on earth will be fulfilled if we yield to God's plan. Our purpose is linked to our gifts, and our gifts are what we offer to others. Our gifts are how we serve.

Married couples should know or at least have an idea of some of the gifts each one brings to the table before the marriage ceremony. In other words, somewhere during the dating season, you have learned some of each other's strengths as well as weaknesses. Indeed, after the wedding has taken place, you hopefully will have a lifetime to help strengthen each other to be the very best versions of yourselves.

Your purpose is also linked to your life's mission. What I have found so far in my life is that your purpose is related to something you like to do anyway. It has to do with your heart, your passion, and your desire. If you like to help people with the right motives, sometimes you are the person that gets hurt the most. But because it's your life's mission to help, you keep right on doing it.

Our purposeful lives are all intertwined in the master plan of God. We should live on purpose, laugh on purpose, and positively influence others on purpose. Sometimes we cannot quite figure out what God was thinking during certain seasons of our lives. However, God's thoughts are not our thoughts.

We sometimes wonder what would have happened if we had not moved to another city, if we had not taken that position at work, if we had not gotten married, or if we had gotten married. And often, we don't have the answers to these questions. But be assured, life would not be life without some regret, because we don't always make the right decisions. However, there is a purpose, even for distress.

If there had not been any pain in my life, I would not be authentic. I wouldn't know how to have compassion for others. I could not step up to the plate to be an encourager. I might not have taken the time or the effort to write the words from my heart to you through these love letters.

Sunshine without rain is not a very good balance. We need rain to survive. Physically speaking, rain is a critical element in the earth's water cycle, which is vital to life on earth. Plants need rain to grow. Animals and humans as well need rain. Spiritually speaking, rain symbolizes time, seasons, and new beginnings. It has a rebirth connection, a cleansing effect. It has its purpose.

The Bible tells us in Genesis 6 that when God saw that evil was out of control, it broke His heart. So, He made a clean sweep of people, animals—the complete works. The first flood had a purpose; the earth was corrupt and filled with violence, and it needed to change. While the Ark was being prepared, the people were allowed to repent. Noah carried the message, but did they believe him? Much like today, many do not believe. But consider this, it is now time for preparation. The critical thing to remember about purpose, is that God judged the world back in the days of Noah. Though He promised there would not be another flood, He will nevertheless judge the world again.

Your life purpose is your contribution. What are you bringing to the table? Are you interested in helping others, teaching others, leading others, encouraging others? Does your passion include music, public speaking, the political arena, sports, or health?

You can use all these skills toward building the kingdom of God, leaving a legacy, and living a life that pleases the Lord. After all, why are we here?

Love,
"the MuM"

Self - Exam Questions:

1. Have I sought the Lord about my godly purpose?
2. Have I tapped into the gifts that make my purpose purposeful?
3. What tools do I lack to recognize why God brought me here?
4. Am I willing to seek mentorship, to help me reach the things God has purposed for me?

Faith Confessions

Father, in the name of the Lord Jesus, I recognize, by faith, that You had me on your mind before the worlds were formed. Thank You for revealing my real purpose. Thank You for helping me realize that You have given me all things that pertain to life and godliness. I will continue to share my purpose with the world as the Holy Spirit leads.

"For success, attitude is equally as important as ability."
- Walter Scott

Letter Nine

DESTINY MOMENTS

Everything has already been decided. It was known long ago what each person would be. So, there's no use arguing with God about your destiny.
Ecclesiastes 6:10 NLT

Dear Beloved,

Scripture teaches that humans are created with the ability to make moral choices and that we are responsible for those choices. Therefore, our destiny depends upon whether we live in harmony with God, following His moral teachings. It is our responsibility to decide our destiny.

You have a part to play in your destiny. The Bible lets you know in Ecclesiastes 3 that there is a time and a season for everything. Birth, death, healing, breaking down, building up, weeping, laughing, are all seasons appointed by God. Knowing your season is vital to the success of your life.

There are times when you just get a feeling that something super vast and exciting is about to happen in your life. It may be after times of pain and disappointment. But there is a particular feeling that comes along with the spirit of expectation that tells you things are about to change.

My husband often says, "Something big is about to happen!" Bishop Wiley says all the time, "God is getting ready to flip the script." Mixed with a little faith these two declarations become war cry chants to a believer. For this reason, we must remain flexible and be at-the-ready to transition from mediocrity into a blessed position.

One of my destiny moments happened while we were stationed in Washington, D.C. back in the 1980s.

I attended business school, taking classes to equip me for a secretarial position upon graduation. That went well. I was blessed to be able to do it full-time, and in just four months, with God's help, I graduated from the program. Job placement was one of my student benefits; I was sent on an interview before I took the final exam. I felt great about the interview and was offered the position. Even though I had the position, which was the reason I was in school, it served as motivation for me also to go ahead and complete the program.

I enjoyed working at the Department of Commerce in the mid-1980s. I got promoted every year for the first four years because the position was a GS-4 target GS-7. That was an attainable goal. I learned from my husband that as soon as you get promoted to start operating at the next grade level.

When you're going about your way in life from day to day, you never know who's watching you or how you are perceived. There was a lady that worked up the hall from me at Commerce; we referred to her as the head secretary. I didn't even think the lady liked me, let alone would recommend me for a position in the private sector. When she did, even one of my close colleagues cautioned me, "Maybe she's setting you up for something." Well, unbeknownst to my colleague and me, the Lord was setting me up for something indeed extraordinary. *When He sets you up, it's a godly setup, so just receive it.* That's what I love about the Lord—even when we think we're not on His mind (which is never), believe me, we are on His mind, and He is definitely up to something great in our lives.

Wow is the only word I can sometimes say when I think about how great and mighty our God is, and how He has our best interest in mind always. It's amazing how He's developing our lives into destiny moments.

I went on that interview at a downtown private law firm with faith, grace, and confidence. I was offered the job, and of course, doubt set in and quickly turned to fear. Remember, they are in the same family. I dared to turn down the job based on those two factors —doubt and fear. The office manager came back with an increased salary offer. I was in my 20s; however, I had enough sense to seek counsel. Though I was fearful, I knew the spirit of fear was not from the Lord. No, I didn't pray for this opportunity; it just came. The question I entertained and the perhaps the issue for you is, what do you do with the unexpected when it comes?

Well, I talked to a good friend who had already made that transition from civil service to the private sector. He told me to make a list of all the pros and cons on a piece of paper to see which held more weight and to just go from there. I quickly took him up on this recommendation because, after all, time was of the essence. Of course, I talked to my husband, who at the time was on temporary duty in Indianapolis, Indiana. Essentially, what he told me was, "take the job; it's your time; it's your season!!!" After prayer and considering the advice presented to me, I took the position, gained the experience, and so much more.

Doubt and fear can prevent you from experiencing your destiny moment. In the end, where do they get you? Not very far. Sometimes you have to step out on faith, believe in yourself, and above all things, believe in God.

Think of it like this, if you have a personal relationship with God, He is, without question, guiding your footsteps. The angel of the Lord is your number one cheerleader. Your marching orders are to step out on faith and silence the enemy and all that would join him in delaying your destiny.

Not only did I weigh the pros and the cons, comparing what I had on the present job and what I was being offered on the new job, but I wrote down a scripture for all the pros. Isaiah 43:18-19 (NKJV) says it best, "Do not remember the former things, Nor consider the things of old. Behold, I will do a new thing, Now it shall spring forth; Shall you not know it? I will even make a road in the wilderness *And* rivers in the desert."

Sometimes we need to know clearly when a chapter in our life has ended, and certainly when a new one is to begin. Letting go is never easy, not for something you are so familiar with, but embracing and accepting the challenge for something brand new is growth and maturity in the making.

I ended up relaunching my government career years later. However, if I had never taken the risk to grow and mature outside of my comfort zone, again, you would not be reading these words right now. Utilizing your faith in God makes life so much easier. After all, how can faith grow if you never use it?

Our Washington, D.C. assignment lasted nine years, which was very much unheard of for military families. Though that area seemed like home, I was very excited to receive those military orders that would send us to Naples, Italy—even so the feeling was bittersweet. We met some of the most beautiful friends in the world who had become family. We bought our first house on this tour, and we had our first child on this tour; however, it was time to grow even more.

By the end of this fascinating chapter in our lives, my close friends could tell I was transforming. I call it going from my caterpillar to my butterfly phase. I was taking my relationship with the Lord seriously. My love for God, as well as my hunger for Him, were daily increasing.

Once we arrived in Naples, it was vital for us to connect with a church. We became a part of the Living Word Christian Fellowship. So, when this happened, I was given Sunday School books and asked to teach the Adult Sunday School class. I had never taught adults and was nervous about the assignment. However, I embraced it and agreed to myself that I was willing to learn everything I could digest. My mother sent me commentaries and other biblical tools to use as study guides. They helped me to break the lessons down and get a better understanding since we were not on the internet just yet. I remember how I would start studying on Sunday nights for the next week's lesson. That is where I discovered my teaching gift. I am still amazed at the fact that the Lord knew it all along. After all, He is the gift-giver, and we all have several gifts. I began to work that gift with the sole purpose of pleasing Him.

The teaching opportunity that began at Living Word led to so many other opportunities. I connected with the Protestant Women of the Chapel (PWOC), for their weekly Bible studies, retreats, Monday muffins orientation to meet the incoming military families, and many other outreach activities, which I very much enjoyed.

Not only did my husband and I grow up in the Lord while in Naples, but our family grew as well. We had our second king there at the U.S. Naval Hospital. He had the most incredible introduction to the world. The doctors and nurses greeted him as soon as he was born with the words, "Hi, Reagan."

Another one of my destiny moments occurred while our family was stationed at Supreme Headquarters Allied Powers of Europe (SHAPE Belgium). I volunteered to accompany our youth group from the chapel on a mission trip from Belgium to the Czech Republic.

When I say it was a long way outside of my comfort zone, I mean, it was something I never expected to do. Not that I was not the "give back to the community" type of person—after all, I was a Brownie and Girl Scout. I volunteered for the American Cancer Society, collecting donations door-to-door in my neighborhood (a task handed down to me from my mother), and I participated in so many church, school, and community activities.

I believe part of the reason this mission trip was so out of my comfort zone was that our sons, Ryan and Reagan, were young guys and were not old enough to be on this project. They stayed home with Dad. So, their Mother volunteered to be with someone else's children. Volunteering to be one of the chaperone's involved certain sacrifices, such as taking forty hours of annual leave from my government job, traveling in a chartered bus for thirteen hours, and being away from my family for a few days. However, I found it not only to be sacrificial but also mentally stimulating.

We had around 20-30 young people and five adult chaperones on this missionary journey. Our living arrangements were similar to the television show *M*A*S*H*, maybe not quite that austere, but far from our comfortable home located in the city of Ghlin. Our mission for the week, besides nightly revival-type services with the locals, was to improve one of the elementary school playgrounds by painting fences and building equipment. Except for attending the revival meetings in the evenings, these activities were totally outside of my comfort zone. But I had such a desire to be a part of something much larger than myself.

Just to see the eyes of the young people light up with joy made it worthwhile being there. Some of the young local little girls touched my hair and face because they probably haven't seen anyone in person that looked like me. That was over 20 years ago, but I will never forget that feeling of showing love and compassion and how it made a massive difference to one community, as well as the fulfillment we all experienced.

Have you ever thought about what you can do that may involve you getting outside of your comfort zone? Perhaps it's the same thing that would make a significant impact on others. I am a firm believer in each one reach one by any means necessary.

Doors continued to open for me again at SHAPE. One of our PWOC instructors was going to be out, and she needed a substitute. No one that was a part of PWOC had heard me teach or even publicly speak for that matter, but I was given the lesson plans and asked to teach the next week. Soon afterward, I became a regular teacher, and I received so much favor on my job. I was allowed to teach the noon hour class and eat my lunch with no work issues at all. I never took that for granted. I was always nervous before the classes, but by the time I returned to my office, I had such a sense of accomplishment. It was so surreal.

I truly thank the Lord for my years as an active duty military spouse. I met so many amazing people and was honored with other spouses at an event hosted by then-First Lady Barbara Bush at Bolling Air Force Base.

I often reflect on the magnificent seasons of my life. I was a civil servant, a private sector employee, a church secretary, a Mary Kay Consultant, a women's ministry chairperson, an event planner, a bible teacher, a college student, an evangelist, a military spouse, a soccer mum, a wife and stay-at-home mum. And I'm just getting started. Through it all, I learned to treasure every step of my journey so far and to keep my trust in God. Each moment became a key part of my destiny.

Love,
"the MuM"

Self - Exam Questions:

1. What is it that I need to rely on God for the most in my life right now?
2. Am I ever guilty of holding up my destiny with doubt and fear? Explain.
3. What are some of the steps to be taken to improve my trust level in God?
4. How can getting outside of my comfort zone help make a difference in my community?
5. How would I like to be remembered? As a risk-taker, or as a person that never bothered to live outside of the box?

Faith Confessions:

I decree and declare that I have the faith, the courage, and the favor of Esther. I thank God for choosing me before the foundation of the world that I should be holy and without blame before Him in love. I thank God I am walking in his ordered steps. The Word of God declares that eyes have not seen, ears have not heard, neither have entered into the heart of man, what the Lord has prepared for me. I will not rush the process; instead, I will trust the process.

"A person often meets his destiny on the road he took to avoid it."
- Jean de La Fontaine

Letter Ten

IT WAS THE BEST OF TIMES AND THE WORST OF TIMES

These things I have spoken unto you, that in me ye might have peace. In the world ye shall have tribulation: but be of good cheer; I have overcome the world.
St. John 16:33

Dear Beloved,

The Bible lets you know in Ecclesiastes 7:14 TM:

On a good day, enjoy yourself;
On a bad day, examine your conscience.
God arranges for both kinds of days
So that we won't take anything for granted."

Father God allows you to experience both good and

bad days. His wisdom is awesome as He mixes them both. His purpose is always to bring the best results to even the darkest days. Don't ever forget God is in control.

We all can agree that the world is ever-changing. It appears that the year 2020 has been the most fearful and the most uncertain times of our life. However, as I reflect on the signs of the times, I am reminded of 2 Timothy 3:1-5, which states:

> *This know also, that in the last days perilous times shall come.*
>
> *For men shall be lovers of their own selves, covetous, boasters, proud, blasphemers, disobedient to parents, unthankful, unholy,*
>
> *Without natural affection, trucebreakers, false accusers, incontinent, fierce, despisers of those that are good,*
>
> *Traitors, heady, high minded, lovers of pleasures more than lovers of God;*
>
> *Having a form of godliness but denying the power thereof: from such turn away.*

The above scripture, also discussed in a previous letter, allows us to see the exact things we are currently experiencing in our society. You do know there is nothing new under the sun, right?

The seasoned Apostle by the name of Paul ministers to the young Pastor Timothy in this passage. I have often wondered how it would be to interview someone from that direct era in biblical times.

So, in my mind, this is what I believe it would be like to interview the Apostle Paul as if he were here today in the 21st Century. These are the highlights of the interview:

Me: Good day Apostle, it's an honor to meet you and

talk to you. Tell me a little about yourself.

Apostle: My name was Saul, and I'm from a town called Tarsus, and if you can believe it, I used to hate Christians, all of them, and I hated everything they stood for. I was a murderer. I killed innocent people.

Me: So how did you reach this point in your journey?

Apostle: I was later renamed Paul after I saw the resurrected Christ on the road called Damascus. What an experience that was, but it was there that I was converted to Christianity.

Me: Your conversion story is impressive. Tell me about your missionary journeys.

Apostle: I thank God for the opportunity to make three long missionary journeys throughout the Roman Empire, planting churches, preaching the gospel, and giving strength and encouragement to early Christians.

Me: Wow. I also understand that you authored many New Testament books of the Bible that govern Christians to this very day. Tell me about writing those books that bring us so much hope.

Apostle: Who from my former life would have believed that of the twenty-seven books in the New Testament, I am credited with the authorship of thirteen of them? Don't get me wrong; I am very proud of my Jewish heritage. I realized that the gospel was for the Gentiles as well as the Jews. Would you agree that this gospel (the good news of our Lord and Savior Jesus Christ) is for everyone that will receive Him?

Me: I am a believer of that statement. What also quickly comes to my mind is 2 Corinthians 4:3-4 where it says, "But if our gospel be hid, it is hid to them that are lost."

Apostle: Amen. I also recognize the importance of mentorship.

Me: Please share.

Apostle: I firmly believe that everyone needs mentorship in their spiritual and professional lives. So, with the help of

God, I equipped the young minister Timothy into a more effective minister of the gospel and empowered him for success. I believe that receiving outstanding mentorship helps you to pour into your proteges, and the cycle continues when your proteges begin the same work.

Me: I think that's wonderful, Apostle. You were used by God to do a great job in the kingdom. There's so much of that needed today as it was in your day as well.

Me: Thanks so much for sharing your heart with my readers. We have gained great insight, and you have encouraged us to be a real blessing to others.

Most believers have their favorite biblical characters, and I can genuinely say that I am so impressed with the Apostle Paul and his accomplishments. I do believe, with all my heart, that's what it would have been like to interview this great servant. I also admire that even at the end of the Apostle's earthly life, he was doing what he did best. He encouraged the saints primarily through letters, as I am encouraging you right now.

Does your sense of urgency match the Apostle's when he references the last days in 2 Timothy? We've heard it so many times; we've sung songs and hymns, and we've talked about the last days, haven't we? But the last days began at Pentecost and will continue until Jesus comes back to get us. Believe me when I say we're living in the last days.

These are the signs of the times. That's the reason we should make the most of our time. There's absolutely no time to be ungodly, no time to be in the dark regarding your salvation, no time to be uncommitted to kingdom business, no time to be selfish, no time to be unloving, and for sure, no time to be unforgiving. There's just no time. You don't have to be very spiritual to see the manifestation of 2 Timothy 3:1-5.

Every time we look at the news, view it on our mobile

devices, or read the newspapers, these actions have become commonplace. Some of us are so immune to it that it doesn't even shake us like unpleasant news used to do.

Am I saying we are supposed to be perfect people, not ever making a single mistake, not ever sinning? No. We all come short of the glory of God at times. However, covenant people don't make sinning a habit. Covenant people know how to repent. Covenant people possess the love that cares and shows patience for the unsaved and the unchurched until they grow spiritually as well.

There are times we should take off our judge's robe, put the gavel down, and judge ourselves. Would you agree that the body of Christ cannot afford to misrepresent God's promises? People everywhere are looking for truth, and we are responsible for sharing God's truth. The Bible clearly states you shall know the truth, and the truth shall make you free.

We are constantly reminded of the difficult times when we reflect on the unrest of our environment, terrorism, senseless shootings, police brutality, and the list goes on and on. But I like what Jesus said in St. John 16:33. In His last moments with His disciples, He provides warnings as well. The warning is "In the world you will have tribulation," but notice how He never leaves us on a low note. He goes on to say, "But be of good cheer." Here comes the promise: "I have overcome the world." He is not saying that I will overcome or that I desire to overcome, but that He has overcome (past tense). Jesus overcoming the world means He has prevailed, He has defeated the darkness of this world, He has conquered Satan, demons, and principalities, and He has conquered all on our behalf. With these words, Jesus told His disciples to take courage.

I discovered something valuable and worth keeping in mind as I encounter life's battles. It's a winning formula: [battle fought + battle won = his peace]. When we reflect on the fact that in Him, we can have His peace, then we can be of good cheer. Good cheer is not something to be experienced only at Christmas time. Good cheer is something that gives us joy and gladness, encouragement, and comfort; it also gives us hope in all seasons of our lives.

It is the worst of times because the Bible warns us of this challenging period. It is the best of times because we are living in the grace dispensation. It is the worst of times because many are the afflictions of the righteous, but it is the best of times because the Lord delivers them out of them all. It is the worst of times because when our hearts are overwhelmed, we plead for Him to lead us to the rock that is higher. But it is the best of times, after all, in the day of trouble, He will conceal us in His tabernacle and in the secret place of His tent, He will hide us. (Ephesians 3, Psalm 34:19, Psalm 27:5).

It is the worst of times because weeping may endure for a night, but it is the best of times because joy comes in the morning. It is the worst of times because the thief comes only to steal, kill, and destroy, but it is the best of times because Jesus said, "I have come that they may have life, and have it more abundantly." It is the worst of times because though I walk through the valley of the shadow of death, but it is the best of times because I will fear no evil, for God is with me. (Psalm 30:5b, St. John 10:10, Psalm 23:4).

It is the worst of times because evildoers came upon me to devour my flesh, but it is the best of times because my adversaries and my enemies—guess what happened? They stumbled and fell. It is the worst of times because the wages of sin are death, but it is the best of times because the gift of God is eternal life in Christ Jesus our Lord. It is the worst of times because our outer self is wasting away, but it is the best of times because our inner self is renewed day by day. It is the worst of times because even the youth shall faint and be weary, and the young men shall utterly fall, but it's the best of times because they that wait upon the Lord shall renew their strength; they shall mount up with wings as eagles, they shall run, and not be weary, and they shall walk and not faint. (Psalm 27:2, Romans 6:23, 2 Corinthians 4:16, Isaiah 40:30-31).

The Bible sums it up Ecclesiastes 12:9-14:

And moreover, because the preacher was wise, he still taught the people knowledge; yea, he gave good heed, and sought out, and set in order many proverbs.

The preacher sought to find out acceptable words: and that which was written was upright, even words of truth.

The words of the wise are as goads, and as nails fastened by the masters of assemblies, which are given from one shepherd.

And further, by these, my son, be admonished: of making many books there is no end; and much study is a weariness of the flesh.

Let us hear the conclusion of the whole matter:

Fear God and keep His commandments, For this is man's all.

For God will bring every work into judgment, Including every secret thing, Whether good or evil.

Love,
"the MuM"

Self - Exam Questions:

1. How do I handle things I cannot control?
2. Am I a chronic complainer?
3. Do I only dwell on the problem, or am I resolution oriented?
4. Do I consult with others when facing adversity, or do I seek God first?
5. How can I better make lemonade from the lemons that life sometimes serves?

Faith Confessions

I stand on the Word of God, according to Psalm 5:12, I walk in His favor all day long. May His favor surround me like a shield. I thank God now for favor and blessings in my life. I thank God for giving me grace. I thank God for His Word that reminds me that He will withhold no good thing from those who do right.

I stand on the Word of God, according to St. Luke 2:52 and Numbers 6:25-26, I am a success today. I have God's special favor upon me today. He makes His face shine upon me today. He is gracious to me today. I expect something extraordinary to happen to me this day.

I stand on the Word of God and declare by faith that as I sit down in His presence, I will be reminded that He's my refuge. I trust Him, and I am safe.

"True happiness is to enjoy the present, without anxious dependence of the future."
-Lucius Annaeus Seneca

Letter Eleven

SPIRITUAL HOUSE CLEANING

*The heart is deceitful above all things, and desperately
wicked: who can know it?*
Jeremiah 17:9

Dear Beloved,

Have you ever just wanted to begin anew? Have you
ever had a goal of getting organized while decluttering your
mind, your home, or your workplace? If you're like me, it
probably leaves you with an excellent feeling to take on
these kinds of projects. No matter if it's spring cleaning, fall
cleaning, or even summer or winter cleaning, tackling the
excess can be overwhelming, but exciting and therapeutic
as well.

Imagine being the CEO of decluttering, and producer
of a stress-free environment. Recently, I reorganized my
kitchen pantry. It was a long overdue project. The key was
to get started. The spirit of procrastination speaks words
like this: "This is too hard," or "This will take too long,"

or "You don't even have time or the energy to do this," or "Wait for someone else to do it." These same words could prevent you from accomplishing anything on your to-do list.

I believe every now and then, it is vital to do a SWOT analysis on yourself. A SWOT analysis is an excellent assessment and planning technique used to help you or your organization identify its strengths (internal), weaknesses (internal), opportunities (external), and threats (external).

Whether you are spiritually house cleaning or not, it's important first of all to not guess, but know your strong areas, and of course, to also know your weak areas. Who are we kidding? Everyone has strengths and weaknesses. You can better understand yourself and why you think and act the way you do, if you are willing and able to identify your strengths and weaknesses.

I believe this is also an excellent place to point out that we have an adversary that has been studying us for years, and from his research, he knows the results of our SWOT analysis matrix. If you're thinking like I'm thinking, that's not exactly fair, so get to know yourself and conduct the research on your adversary.

Know what is happening in your life that allows you to be even keeled or what causes you to be topsy-turvy. That's why it's so important to know yourself. Though you are ever-changing, believe in yourself, and consider what God says about you.

You will find this tool useful in your spiritual life as well, specifically, in determining your spiritual condition. When there is something physically wrong, you, like many others, will seek medical help. However, the question is, how do you know, and what do you do when something is going wrong in your spiritual life? For instance, is there a pastor or spiritual leader? Is there a counselor? Is there someone close to you that's also close to God? In other words, who is your spiritual covering?

As you journey through life to find you, ask yourself the question, "What is going on inside of my heart?" What about the inside of your heart? I like the passage from this version; the answer is provided in Jeremiah 17:9-10 (TM) we read, "The heart is hopelessly dark and deceitful, a puzzle that no one can figure out, But I, God, search the heart and examine the mind. I get to the heart of the human. I get to the root of things. I treat them as they are, not as they pretend to be."

That's it; God gets to the heart of the human. That is just where we need Him to be. I have heard people say for many years, "God knows my heart." There has never been a more factual statement. He does know your heart. That's just like taking your vehicle to the shop for repair. Many people make excuses for taking the car somewhere other than where it was made. But wouldn't the creator or the maker know the product inside and out?

If you're a baker and you made an old-fashioned pound cake, you know that the recipe calls for 1 cup unsalted butter, 2 cups all-purpose flour, 2 cups granulated sugar, and 6 large eggs. So, if someone insists that there's a pineapple taste to your cake, and you know beyond a shadow of a doubt that you didn't include pineapple in your recipe, you can easily disregard what someone else thinks. If God knows what He placed inside of us, and He does, everyone else's thoughts and opinions can be easily ignored.

Since we put time and effort into cleaning our natural surroundings, there is also a need to do some "spiritual house cleaning" as well. In 1 Timothy 4:8 (TM) we read, "Workouts in the gymnasium are useful, but a disciplined life in God is far more so, making you fit both today and forever."

In our society, much value is placed on the physical. It's always great to be conscious of becoming fit, maintaining physical fitness, and experiencing good health. We also know that our physical health is susceptible to disease and injury. We should always remember that our body is the temple of the Holy Spirit. It's where God lives. We should keep the temple in excellent condition.

Equally important is how we should maintain spiritually. To develop our spiritual muscles, we must build our faith and train ourselves to be godly, and we do that by the Word of God.

That frightens some people to no end. Train me to be like God? The flesh does not want to be like God. The flesh just wants to remain like it is. Training and developing faith? No. Are you willing to make the sacrifice to discipline yourself to get spiritually fit?

There is one thing for sure; you cannot do this alone. The Bible provides much encouragement to us when it instructs us to draw close to God and allow our hearts and bodies to be cleansed.

The first step in our home cleaning project, since we have no way of cleaning ourselves, is to draw near to God and ask Him to do the cleaning. God will meet any need. Just simply ask Him. He knows what we need even before the prayer is prayed.

Most children do not have a problem asking their parents for things they need, or even something they want, and our children know us through our relationship. God wants us to approach Him as little children, with childlike faith through our relationship with Him. If you desire a clean heart, ask Him to help you.

David did not have a problem with asking God to assist. His plea according to Psalm 51:10 to the Lord was, "Create in me a clean heart, O God, and renew a right spirit within me." After we have prayed for guidance, we need to let the true work begin... the cleaning. The keyword here is "renew." Everyone loves "the new"—a new journey, a new career, a new house, a new car, the New Year, or a new opportunity.

Well, give yourself permission to accept the new you that the Lord will develop—if only the old you will allow Him to do the work. David prayed this prayer after committing adultery with Bathsheba, having her husband killed, and then covering it all up. Of course, his actions were wrong, and David repented of his sins. We should do likewise when we sin. Also, the Word tells us in Hebrews 10:22, "Let us draw near with a true heart in full assurance of faith, having our hearts sprinkled from an evil conscience, and our bodies washed with pure water."

Maybe you feel you've gone too far down the wrong road, and there's no way to get back. Well, if that's your true feeling, you have been misled. There is a way back home, and it's through God's Son, Jesus. He will clean you with hyssop and restore you to His original plan for your life.

Love,
"the MuM"

Self - Exam Questions:

1. The Bible tells us in St. Matthew 15:19 (NIV), "For out of the heart come evil thoughts--murder, adultery, sexual immorality, theft, false testimony, slander." In the midst of all of the heart issues, how can I experience the mind of Christ?
2. What kinds of things can I do to polish my thought life?
3. Does my current relationship with the Lord allow me to come clean with him and let him know what I need?
4. What are my strengths?
5. What are my weaknesses?

Faith Confessions

Lord, help me to daily feast on your Word and allow the Holy Spirit to work in my life. Help me to clean up everything that is not according to your will and your way. Lord, I thank you for the solution found in Psalm 24:4 that says, "He that hath clean hands, and a pure heart; who hath not lifted up his soul unto vanity, nor sworn deceitfully."

"Do not take life too seriously. You will never get out of it alive."
- Elbert Hubbard

Letter Twelve

LIGHT OVER DARKNESS

~~~~♡~~~~

For there is nothing hidden that will not be disclosed,
and nothing concealed that will not be known or
brought out into the open.
St. Luke 8:17 NIV

Dear Beloved,

I thought about it long and hard. Where are we going with this letter? What exactly is meant by light over darkness? Is it skin color? No. Is light and dark in competition? No. Is one preferred over the other? Maybe.

As mentioned in previous letters, God has a divine purpose for everything. Very early on from the creation story, we can find a familiar scripture passage that lets us know God did not allow light and darkness to co-exist. God saw the need to divide the light from the darkness. Keep in mind, everything can be seen in the light, but those same things are not easily viewed or recognized in darkness. On the first day of creation, darkness was dispelled when God created light.

The Word of God informs us in Genesis 1:1-4:

In the beginning, God created the heaven and the earth. And the earth was without form, and void; and darkness was upon the face of the deep. And the Spirit of God moved upon the face of the waters. And God saw the light, and it was good; and God divided the light from the darkness.

How many times have we heard the old saying, "What's done in the dark will come to light?" I grew up hearing this phrase quite often, not knowing what was meant by it. I used to wonder, is it just a saying. I have found the expression to be true. Its meaning comes from the fact that secrets or hidden things eventually surface to full exposure. The light always exposes darkness. What's the idea of hiding things? What's the concept of deception? Who taught you how to cheat?

When you think about it, we only hide things we don't want anyone to know. Usually, because it's things we know are wrong, and we also know someone is going to check us, call us out, or judge us.

The nighttime used to be a time when crimes were committed, and bad things happened, but sin is presently running so rampant; evil has no regard for timing. No longer are crimes waiting to be conducted during the darkness, but rapes, murders, human trafficking, arsons, burglaries, robbery, drug deals, and more are all now taking place in the light of day.

One of my favorite childhood games was hide-and-seek. Perhaps you have played it or at least know how it's played. Anyway, in this top-rated children's game, one player closes his or her eyes for a brief period (often counting to 50 or whatever number is agreed on—we never made it even close to 50), while the other players hide. The seeker then opens his eyes and tries to find the hiders; the first one found is the next seeker, and the last is the winner of the round.

This game was played in my neighborhood strictly for fun. We didn't realize the physical benefits being gained. We didn't even know we were getting a good workout, running, thinking, and building stamina while our muscles developed. We had no idea, nor did we have any concern about the challenges involved in squeezing into the perfect hiding place that would help improve our balance, agility, and coordination. It helped us to be competitive and it created a unique bond that extends well into our adult lives.

However, the concept behind the game can also be viewed as spiritual. We are primarily searchers by nature. We read books and we search the internet, we attend classes, with one goal, to find the truth. That is the reason you always need to be yourself; people can receive from you more readily if you are genuine and transparent. Truth seekers want to know, has anyone been through what I'm going through. If so, how did you come out of it?

On my spiritual journey, I have encountered people who simply want to stay in "hide mode." Perhaps you have witnessed the same. I have discovered those who seemingly enjoyed being a part of mega ministries for the sole purpose of being a part of the fellowship but not being easily found. They didn't want to get to know anyone in the ministry, and they didn't want anyone to get to know them. That also kept their spiritual leaders as well as the parishioners from knowing what gifts they had to offer. They took what appeared to be the easy route, as they hid in the crowd.

You would probably agree that these kinds of people suffer from accountability issues. In any relationship, accountability is necessary. Being accountable is essential in marriage, in business, in employment, in ministry, and the list goes on. I want to emphasize being accountable is especially important between you and your pastor. Most people do not realize that your pastor watches over your soul, according to Hebrews 13:17. If you're walking in the light let's be clear, learn to embrace the value of accountability.

The truth is, we were all lost. If not, the Savior would have found no one to save. "For the Son of man is come to seek and to save that which was lost," St. Luke 19:10. God says in Jeremiah 29:13, "And ye shall seek me, and find me, when ye shall search for me with all your heart." That's wonderful news. We are not seeking a Father that is hiding from His children. We can never accuse God of child neglect. Never.

The object of the game of hide-and-seek is to be sought, but not caught. While playing the game as a child, we all wanted to be that person who ran to touch the base without the seeker, even having a clue about our place of escape. Sometimes we carry that same set of rules in our personal, spiritual, and professional lives.

As we grow and mature into adulthood, we tend to hide more things than we need to hide. Granted, you cannot share everything with everybody; I get that. But if you don't share the right stuff—the unpleasant things, the disappointments, the rejections—with the right person, at the right time, it could cause the wheels of your wagon to explode.

Now you're at a low point, the point where the adversary loves you (not really), but he only appears to be in love with you. Your adversary acts happy with you because he knows you are going to pay him some attention. He will talk to you. You will communicate back to him. It's guaranteed that he will get in your mind and cause thoughts that you would not typically experience.

When he has your ear, he will fill it with a bunch of lies such as:

No one loves you.

No one cares about you. Don't even try.

Don't go back.

Don't pick up the phone. Don't apologize.

Don't forgive.

None of the things the adversary tells you about yourself or others is accurate. How do I know this? Because the Bible lets us know in St. John 8:44 the adversary is not only a liar, but he is the father of lies.

The solution to this dilemma is not to hide from but to seek the Lord. Psalm 34:10 (NKJV) says, "The young lions lack and suffer hunger; but those who seek the Lord shall not lack any good thing."

Don't stay in darkness for too long. Have you ever noticed how depressing it is not to allow any sunlight into your home? Have you ever noticed how you felt when your curtains were drawn, and blinds closed tight? It could signify that your mind and your spirit are also closed. But suddenly, the world changes when you allow the natural sunlight to come in. It's the difference between a frown and a smile, a hug, and a push away. When you realize that you need to let the sunshine in, perhaps you will also know you need the "Son," the Lord Jesus Christ, to shine in your life.

We need to let our light shine and inspire others to do the same. We cannot do it alone, however, it is the job of the Holy Spirit to lead, guide and teach. It is refreshing to know we have the help needed, and we are never alone.

When light is exposed, darkness does not have a choice. In other words, when the truth is revealed, no matter what it is—family secrets, adulterers' affairs, or broken promises—freedom comes, and bondages are over. That's a good reason to keep things on the up and up with God. He knows everything about you anyway, so why lie to Him?

If you're a parent, uncle, aunt, or have children or millennials around you at any time, you know how it would feel for the young person you are spiritually covering, and physically taking care of to deceive you. It doesn't feel good at all. Deception is not of God, and it's not something you want in your life.

First Thessalonians 5:5 tells us, "Ye are all the children of light, and the children of the day: we are not of the night, nor of darkness." First John 2:8 says, "Again, a new commandment I write unto you, which thing is true in him and in you: because the darkness is past, and the true light now shineth." Jesus speaks in St. John 8:12 declaring, "I am the light of the world: he that followeth me shall not walk in darkness but shall have the light of life."

Now just so you won't get it twisted, if you think you can walk in the light and have hatred in your heart, again, you're deceiving yourself. First John 4:20 lets us know by the same token; you cannot say you love God and hate your sister or brother. You do know that all of your sisters and brothers are not biologically related to you, right? I am your sister. The man that just passed you in the store is your brother.

There is an old saying, and it's still true that you cannot be so heavenly minded until you are no earthly good. Though earth is not our permanent home, we must make the most of our time and opportunities while we are here. If you are a child of God, that's an indication that you are a child of the light, and that you do not walk in darkness.

If ever the world needed help with walking in the light, walking in integrity, and walking in truth, it sure is right now. With God's help, we can get it done. We can shine like stars in the sky. Keep in mind; it's not a one-time deal. We need to be consistently refueled like a vehicle.

Someone asked me recently, "Do you go to church on Wednesdays?" Since I just met this person, I went easy on her, but I wondered how in the world could a person only fill up their tank once a week and survive? Should I say more? Going to church is like going to a gas station. If you're like me, you can hardly wait for a high-tech word. When the benediction is given, you can go out and strive to reach the next level in your faith, which is an attainable goal.

Love,
"the MuM"

Self - Exam Questions:

1. When I think about darkness, what is the first thing that pops into my mind? Why?
2. How can I live in the light of God?
3. How can I be a good representative of God's light?
4. Am I a person of integrity?
5. Am I too quick to judge a situation?

Faith Confessions

Thank you, Lord, for your Word that reminds me that I am a chosen generation, a royal priesthood, a holy nation, a peculiar people; that I should shew forth the praises of Him who hath called me out of darkness into His marvelous light. Lord, thank you that your Word is a lamp for my feet, a light on my path. Thank you for allowing me to let my light shine before others that they may see your good deeds and glorify you in Heaven.

"Nothing can stop the man with the right mental attitude from achieving his goal; nothing on earth can help the man with the wrong mental attitude."
- Thomas Jefferson

Letter Thirteen

HOW TO BE AN ENCOURAGER

Anxiety weighs down the heart, but a kind word cheers it up.
Proverbs 12:25 NIV

Dear Beloved,

How would you like to be an incredible encourager? How much would you appreciate the fact that years from now, someone who you have impacted testifies that you helped them along the way? Perhaps they still remember the things you taught them and the life you displayed. I don't know about you, but I cannot think of a greater reward. If we're going to be that kind of encouragement to others, there are a few things you need to remember.

If you want to be an incredible encourager, first, you need to remember that people are hurting far more than you would ever know and far more than they would ever really show. That means that the person in the office or cubicle next to yours could be smiling through the tears.

Or the person sitting beside you in worship services that looks great, but if you followed them home, perhaps you would see a different person.

How about that person in front of you as you ordered your favorite coffee or tea product? They look great too, but does their true story remain untold? Yes, it does. Or how about if you run into a classmate or a former colleague and reconnect; they tell you life's been just too wonderful, but you find out it's been just the opposite? It's not accurate to say everyone that crosses your path is hurting or distressed, but it is correct to say that there are hurting people among us, much closer than you think. Hurt people hurt people, and until healing is evident, the cycle will continue.

If there's one thing I have learned on my journey, you would be surprised, shocked, and amazed at the situations our brothers and sisters face. You never know what someone is going through, what they have been through, or what trial will be presented next. So, compassion is the call of the day.

Let's face it, we all hurt sometimes, but the good news is what Jesus said in St. Mark 2:17. Jesus says those who are well don't need a physician. Imagine that. Jesus came for the hurt; He came for the pain. There is nothing that we can go through that Jesus did not already go through.

Encouragement was birthed through pain and heartaches; it makes perfect sense. Encouraging is simply the act of providing support and giving someone hope. Again, we all need it; however, there appears not to be quite enough of it. It would be great if we could bottle up encouragement and place it on the market for sale, but unfortunately, that cannot be done. The only way the gift of encouragement continues to be operable and continues to bless others is when someone has an obedient spirit, steps up to the plate, and is willing to share hope with others.

From the time we are born, I believe there is an inner mechanism that longs to be encouraged and fulfilled with strength. I recall the many football and basketball pep rallies during my high school days. Those were enjoyable times. The pep rallies were just as exciting as the games. The whole purpose of a pep rally was aimed at encouraging school spirit, supporting the team members, and inspiring enthusiasm. It was never a time of defeat, it was never a time of doubt, but it was designed to be a time where confidence, drive, and determination were all displayed. It didn't matter if you had not won a game that entire season; the pep rally was a time of celebration in anticipation of a victory. Are you anticipating a victory? Maybe it would not be a bad idea to have a pep rally for yourself, because it's not every day you receive encouragement from someone else.

1 Samuel 30 records a story of how David was faced with a great tragedy of losing families and even being stoned himself. David's soldiers began to turn against him and even talked about killing him. The Bible lets us know David found strength in God's Word, and when adversities came, instead of looking for someone or something to blame, he looked within.

We should also consider this same practice as we go about trying to get issues resolved. David consulted God first to see if he would even win this battle. Seeking God first is critical and encouraging and strengthening yourself is imperative to your spiritual being. Sometimes our flesh does not want to seek God first, but as the story goes, after David prayed to God, the answer came to "go after them." When consulting God, all you need to know is the answer will come, and your faith will be strengthened through the process.

Every team needs an encourager. Barnabus was such a person in the New Testament. Barnabus was a missionary as well as a teacher. His story is told in the book of Acts. His mission was to serve church leaders in whatever was needed. His service resulted in a significant number of people being brought to the Lord.

I am very thankful that the Lord uses me to encourage during this season. Twenty-first century ministry involves encouragement provided through a variety of ways; we're not limited to just phone calls and cards, but sending emails, text messages, or placing encouraging messages on social media. No matter how you do it, do it.

Being an encourager involves being obedient to the Holy Spirit. Whenever the Holy Spirit leads me to send encouragement to someone, I try my best to obey. It always works because, usually, the recipient will respond to me and let me know just how much those words of support helped them at that exact moment they read my message.

Even if you don't receive that type of response, keep on obeying. As the encourager, all you have to know is the Lord is counting on you to make someone's day better.

Are you willing to go the distance? One of my mother's favorite sayings is "What goes around comes around," and believe me, one day; you will need the same support you provided for others. It comes back.

Love,
"the MuM"

Self - Exam Questions:

1. For others: How many people have I encouraged this week?
2. For myself: How can I be more conscious of this simple task?
3. For myself: What makes me tick?
4. For myself: What keeps me going when I need encouragement?
5. For myself: How can I be more aware of when someone needs an extra boost without going overboard?

Faith Confessions

I decree and declare that as I cast my burdens on the Lord, He continues to sustain me. I thank Him for giving power to the weak, and to those who have no might, I thank Him for increasing strength. I thank Him for His Word that reminds me that He never permits the righteous to be moved. I thank the Lord for helping me to inspire others with courage. I am an advocate for sharing my joy.

"If your actions inspire others to dream more, learn more, do more, and become more, you are a leader."
John Quincy Adams

Letter Fourteen

THINK BEFORE YOU SPEAK AND SPEAK IN LOVE

Death and life are in the power of the tongue, And those who love it will eat its fruit.
Proverbs 18:21 NKJV

Dear Beloved,

God tells us in His Word that the tongue has incredible power. We can use our tongue to bring blessings in our lives, or we can use the same tongue to bring curses and death. In other words, we can use our tongue to our advantage or to our disadvantage. When I was growing up, we had a saying, "Sticks and stones can break my bones, but words will never hurt me." However, I found out later in life that the phrase is simply not correct. Your tongue can be the most challenging thing to control and leave you with the most regret, if you use your words to hurt. But there is hope! The Bible tells us that with the help of the Holy Spirit, we can have power and control over our tongue.

The scriptures below provide instructions on the positive use of the tongue, and what God hates. We are encouraged to start speaking words of life and healing beginning right now.

For he that will love life, and see good days, let him refrain his tongue from evil, and his lips that they speak no guile.
-1 Peter 3:10

Let your speech be always with grace, seasoned with salt, that ye may know how ye ought to answer every man.
- Colossians 4:6

Let no corrupt communication proceed out of your mouth, but that which is good to the use of edifying, that it may minister grace unto the hearers.
- Ephesians 4:29

For by thy words thou shalt be justified, and by thy words, thou shalt be condemned.
- St. Matthew 12:37

These six things doth the LORD hate: yea, seven are an abomination unto him: A proud look, a lying tongue, and hands that shed innocent blood, An heart that deviseth wicked imaginations, feet that be swift in running to mischief, A false witness that speaketh lies, and he that soweth discord among brethren.
- Proverbs 6:16-19

He that covereth a transgression seeketh love; but he that repeateth a matter separateth very friends.
- Proverbs 17:9

Set a watch, O LORD, before my mouth; keep the door of my lips.
- Psalm 141:3

We are provided instructions in the Word of God on the tremendous task of taming the tongue and how to simply live well and live wisely: James 3:1-18 (TM) says,

Don't be in any rush to become a teacher, my friends. Teaching is highly responsible work. Teachers are held to the strictest standards. And none of us is perfectly qualified. We get it wrong nearly every time we open our mouths. If you could find someone whose speech was perfectly true, you'd have a perfect person, in perfect control of life.

A bit in the mouth of a horse controls the whole horse. A small rudder on a huge ship in the hands of a skilled captain sets a course in the face of the strongest winds. A word out of your mouth may seem of no account, but it can accomplish nearly anything—or destroy it! It only takes a spark, remember, to set off a forest fire. A careless or wrongly placed word out of your mouth can do that. By our speech we can ruin the world, turn harmony to chaos, throw mud on a reputation, send the whole world up in smoke and go up in smoke with it, smoke right from the pit of hell.

This is scary: You can tame a tiger, but you can't tame a tongue— it's never been done. The tongue runs wild, a wanton killer. With our tongues we bless God our Father; with the same tongues we curse the very men and women he made in his image. Curses and blessings out of the same mouth!

My friends, this can't go on. A spring doesn't gush fresh water one day and brackish the next, does it? Apple trees don't bear strawberries, do they? Raspberry bushes don't bear apples, do they? You're not going to dip into a polluted mud hole and get a cup of clear, cool water, are you?

Do you want to be counted wise, to build a reputation for wisdom? Here's what you do: Live well, live wisely, live humbly. It's the way you live, not the way you talk, that counts. Mean-spirited ambition isn't wisdom. Boasting that you are wise isn't wisdom. Twisting the truth to make yourselves sound wise isn't wisdom. It's the furthest thing from wisdom—it's animal cunning, devilish conniving. Whenever you're trying to look better than others or get the better of others, things fall apart and everyone ends up at the others' throats.

Real wisdom, God's wisdom, begins with a holy life and is characterized by getting along with others. It is gentle and reasonable, overflowing with mercy and blessings, not hot one day and cold the next, not two-faced. You can develop a healthy, robust community that lives right with God and enjoy its results only if you do the hard work of getting along with each other, treating each other with dignity and honor.

We have heard it said so many times that the tongue, while being the smallest member, carries the most considerable weight. Keep in mind that a wise man doesn't get wisdom from not making mistakes; a wise person gains wisdom, sometimes, from putting his foot in his mouth and getting more than full from it.

You can always ask someone for forgiveness when you have said something to hurt them. However, you cannot erase the words you spoke. Though you're not rehearsing them daily, there are times when those words—the enemy will make sure—will come back to mind. Quickly recognize and be determined that you are going to make your words count, and they will bring glory to God.

We can use words to be positive. I will never forget how I used to look in the mirror, and introduce myself as someone with a graduate degree. I would say "Gwendolyn Cody-Davis has an MBA (Master of Business Administration) from (whatever University I felt like naming that day)." I didn't even have an Associate Degree when I made those confessions. But I made a positive faith confession every time I thought about my future and what I wanted to accomplish.

I said it enough times that I believed that, someday, I would get there. There was also a season where I had to put the work in to make my dream come true. Even then, I felt like I would succeed in reaching my goals. I continued to confess, after all, I was speaking life. I took it a step further. When I started my college program, I found a picture of a graduate with a cap and gown on, and I placed the face of my image on the graduation attire. It all started from making an indestructible deliberate faith confession.

As believers, we should only quote what the Word of God says for every situation, which is always accurate, and it is always positive. Meaning that for everything you go through there is a coming out resolution found in the Word of God. Psalm 119:114 became my mantra. The Word of God informed me that He is my hiding place as well as my shield. My hope is in His word. I begin to speak it, meditate on it, and more importantly, walk in it.

I would recommend that you never speak anything contrary to what the Word of God says for your life. Have you ever noticed how quickly your thoughts become words and then promptly develop into actions? Am I saying that every action began as a thought? Indeed, this is what I am saying. The thought was the seed. The seed was planted, but in what kind of ground? If the seed (idea) is planted and grown in the good soil (the Word of God), then it will reap an excellent harvest.

Proverbs 17:27 (NIV) says, "The one who has knowledge uses words with restraint, and whoever has understanding is even-tempered." In other words, whoever restrains his words has a coolness and a calmness. This passage reminds me of our 44th President of the United States,

Barack Obama. With a composed nature, he spoke peace to volatile situations. A relaxed nature is beneficial in a powerful position because it challenges the forces of darkness that would try to offer you a haughty or arrogant spirit instead.

We can take spoken words a step further; it's just not what we say, but it also how we say it. You may speak to someone with a harsh tone, and that could cancel every word you are communicating. If you are ever the victim of receiving harsh words, observe your response. I'm certainly not saying to allow others to beat you up with their words while you remain passive as if you don't matter. On the contrary, you now have the control. When it's your turn to speak, and you manifest a calm demeanor, and the words coming from your mouth come off as from an intelligent, anointed powerhouse, it makes the other person look not so bright.

That's not always the easiest thing to do. Because truthfully speaking, when someone fires off at the mouth with us, we want to fire back doubly so. Not that we're in the business of making others look simple, but if that's anyone's job, let the speaker make himself look simple.

Research shows the average person speaks at least 7,000 words a day. You are known by your words; they do define you. In other words, you are what you say.

Remember the old saying that it is better to keep your mouth shut and appear stupid than to open it and remove all doubt. Proverbs 17:28 (NKJV) tells us, "Even a fool is counted wise when he holds his peace; When he shuts his lips, he is considered perceptive."

Well, just what does the Bible mean when it says we should speak the truth in love? I am so glad you asked that question. Ephesians 4:15 (NKJV) states, "But, speaking the truth in love, may grow up into Him in all things, which is the head even Christ."

In this context—of church unity and spiritual maturity—the Apostle Paul emphasizes rather than be spiritually immature and easily deceived, we are highly encouraged to speak the truth to each other with love, and the reason for this is so we can all grow in maturity. We are to train one another in truth—the foundational gospel truths, truths about who God is and what He has called us to do, hard truths of correction—and guess what motivates us to make this happen? Love. The "love" referred to in this verse is *agape* love, a self-sacrificial love that works for the benefit of the loved one.

We should only speak the truth. The truth always builds up. The truth builds people, dreams, visions, and hope.

It is essential to be careful of the words that come from your mouth and to be responsible for what you say as well. In other words, the Apostle Paul encourages anyone with a tongue, instead of allowing the atmosphere to manifest corruption or even more pollution with your comments, think before you speak.

Ephesians 4:29-32 says, "Let no corrupt communication proceed out of your mouth, but that which is good to the use of edifying, that it may minister grace unto the hearers. And grieve not the Holy Spirit of God, whereby ye are sealed unto the day of redemption. Let all bitterness, and wrath, and anger, and clamor, and evil speaking, be put away from you, with all malice: And be ye kind one to another, tenderhearted, forgiving one another, even as God for Christ's sake hath forgiven you."

In understanding the full meaning of what the Apostle Paul meant, you must realize that the Body of Christ must build up each other. The words that you speak have creative power. Again, you should use your words to build up and not tear down. If you use positive language to benefit situations, then what is the issue here?

The issue is unwholesome communication is not a good idea. If something is unwholesome it is not healthy at all.

Why would you want to knowingly entertain anything corrupt, unsound, or shady? Conduct this test; if the person you are talking about negatively was in the room, would you have the same conversation, same gestures, and same emotions as you would as if they were nowhere around? If the answer is yes, I must ask you to take the same energy and show compassion and try to understand the person you are discrediting.

I believe we have reached the point in time where living in constant fellowship with God is not optional; it is mandatory. The lie that we do not have to confess our sins to God, the lie that it is okay to stay on the same plateau in our spiritual lives, the lie that you can live any way you choose or say anything you feel to anyone, again, all lies. We have to stay in tune with God. It's been said that the Body of Christ, the believers, the church itself, is an organization that sometimes injures its wounded. If you know someone is already wounded—and if the truth be told, we have all been there—then why would you add to the wound, especially with unkind words?

If you cannot handle words, keep silent. We must give an account of our words, good and bad. Not only should you think before speaking, sometimes you should consider thinking instead of talking. Just be silent; it's okay.

Proverbs 15:4 reminds us, "A wholesome tongue is a tree of life: but perverseness therein is a breach in the spirit."

When you reflect on the fact that everyone is essential to God, if you're a God pleaser, everyone should be important to you. You wouldn't want to crush anyone's spirit. Ask the Lord to give you the right words in every situation—words that will bring healing, and most of all, grace to the hearers.

Love,
"the MuM"

Self - Exam Questions:

1. Is talking too much my weakness?
2. Have I thought or said something today contrary to what the word of God says?
3. How can I improve upon the word game?
4. On average, do my words build up or tear down others?
5. How important are my spoken words to me?
6. How can I build up my relationships with the right words?

Faith Confessions

I decree and declare 1 Peter 4:17 that says, "For the time *is come* that judgment must *begin* at the house of God: and if *it* first begin at us, what shall the end *be* of them that obey not the gospel of God?" I decree and declare that my words will reflect only what God's Word says. I decree and declare that I will remain calm in all situations. I thank God for setting a watch before my mouth and keeping the door of my lips, according to Psalm 141:3. God's Word says that I am more than a conqueror through him that loved us; God's Word says that I am the head and not the tail; God's Word says whoever says to this mountain, be removed and be cast into the sea, and does not doubt in his heart, but believes that those things he says will come to pass, he will have whatever he says. I decree and declare that because of my positive words that line up with God's Word; I will have whatever I say.

"Wise men speak because they have something to say;
Fools because they have to say something."
- Plato

Letter Fifteen

HAVE YOU EVER FELT LIKE A NOBODY?

You do matter.

❦

Being confident of this very thing, that He who has begun a good work in you will complete it until the day of Jesus Christ.
Philippians 1:6 NKJV

Dear Beloved,

Have you ever been in an organization or even in a family structure that did not believe in you? Have you ever been in a place where you felt you did not belong? Have you ever felt hated for no reason at all, or you just couldn't pinpoint the real cause you were intensely disliked?

On a scale of 1-10, have you ever felt like a 0? Seriously, have you ever felt like the blockhead character of the comic strip *Peanuts, Charlie Brown*, who was never fully trusted—the one who always got the rock? Have you ever felt like a nobody? Were you the one who was considered to be the weakest link? Were you the one who were projected not to amount to anything in life? Were you the one who was not considered to be of any value to society or anyone?

If you answered yes to any of these questions, this letter is for you. There is probably no better feeling than to have and know people that believe in you. Let's face it; everyone wants to be accepted.

Webster's dictionary defines a nobody as someone unimportant. But who fits that description? God made everybody, which means you are important to Him, so who in the world told you that you were unimportant? Who told you that you don't matter? Those are words spoken from an adversary that does not want you to know who you are and how much work went into your very being.

There are two sides to every story, and this one is no exception. Perhaps you are the one who listened to the wrong voice within your inner space, the voice that told you no one loves you, that no one cares, and that you do not matter. Do you think that God wasted His time thinking you up, growing you up, placing His Spirit inside of you, and after all of that, you don't matter to Him? Not true, once again. If you have ever thought like that, and I'm sure all of us are guilty of this kind of thinking at times, then your mind needs to be transformed quickly.

The other side of the story speaks of the person that has been bullied. Keep in mind; children are not the only ones who get bullied. Adults sometimes get bullied as well. Watch out for people who try to transform you into the person they want you to be. Perhaps the reason they want to do this is that they always want to have control over you. They will appear to be an encourager, cheering you on, praying for you always; however, feeling that they have the upper hand and making you feel inferior could be the goal. In other words, they appear to be your well-wisher, but instead, they wish you would not succeed at all. Don't take the bait. God did not waste His time on His creation. He didn't make any junk. He made every one of us with a divine purpose to be like Him.

Rejection is a painful process that can paralyze your spirit. It can prevent you from moving forward in your life. Usually, a person gets stuck right where they got hurt. Rejection is a Latin word meaning thrown back. Who wants to be thrown around, cast out, not accepted, declined, disapproved, or not selected? If you have ever seen or heard these words, you were probably made to feel as if you weren't good enough.

To the brain, neurologists say experiencing rejection is just like experiencing physical pain. That is the reason rejection hurts so severely. But the good news is found in Hebrews 4:15a. It says, Jesus is not a high priest who is unable to sympathize with our weakness. Jesus was rejected by his family members, by his community, and by people who once claimed to love him. Oh, how   He knows all about rejection. Oh, how He cares about the rejected. The scripture lets us know that Jesus cares.

Let me use a baseball analogy to illustrate my point. Picture this: It's the ninth inning, and the opposing team has a 4-3 lead over the home team. The home team is at-bat with the tying run at third base, the go-ahead run on second base, and first base is empty. The next batter is a slugger—statistically, someone most likely to score the winning run to end the game. The on-deck batter is a marginal hitter, someone least likely to hit the ball or score a run. Given the scenario, the advantage goes to the home team, but the opposing team isn't ready to concede. In a surprise attempt to reverse the odds of losing the game, the opposing team (symbolically, the enemy) intentionally elects to walk the slugger to load the bases because they'd rather pitch to the on-deck batter—the marginal hitter!

So, the stage is set. The marginal batter steps into the batter's box and the play resumes. The pitcher sends the first pitch right down the middle of the plate. With one magical swing of the bat, the marginal hitter sends the first pitch 450 feet into the air over the wall to score a walk-off home run. Do you see the picture? Not only did the marginal hitter bring in the winning run, but he brought in three additional runs to win the game dramatically. The opposing team's thinking was that the moment would be too big for the marginal hitter to have success. That is the game of baseball; and whether you have played before or ever intend to, we are all in the game of life.

Have you ever felt like the marginal hitter? Has anyone ever counted you out? It's not a good feeling to be last in the reality in which we live, and it's also not good to feel that your team cannot count on you. Keep your head up. Why? Because that's where your help always comes from.

When I was in elementary school, everyone wanted to be the line leader. To lead symbolizes accomplishment; it also suggests a position of advantage. You must be smart, creative, and a favored person to be a leader, right? The Bible declares in Deuteronomy 28:13a that the Lord will make us the head and not the tail. But it doesn't end there. We also find in St. Matthew 20:16a that the last shall be first.

We all are valuable to God. We must remember that man does not perceive us in the same way God does. We must also not forget that man did not make us. God did. The Psalmist declares, "We are His people and the sheep of His pasture." If you know you are His, and He made you, would you take everyone else's word over His Word? Who forgave you and saved you? You won't find a person on earth that loves you like the Lord. No wonder God wants to be number one in your life and not further down the list. Remember, He is a jealous God.

I hope that these words will encourage you who have been considered the weakest link. The good news is that you are somebody in Jesus. Go after your dreams with a tenacity that you never had before. Not only did God make you in His image, but He also designed you to be you, to be different, and to know you have value and purpose.

In the Gospel of St. Luke, a story is told about a man called Zacchaeus. The two things that defined Zacchaeus were his small stature and his career as a chief tax-collector at Jericho. Those who collected taxes, of course, were not the most popular people in town. Zacchaeus was a rich man, and the internal revenue agent of his time. He was also a traitor to his nation. On this particular day, he arrived before the crowd so he could see Jesus. Zacchaeus ended up running ahead and climbing a sycamore tree along Jesus's path. Who does that?

As destiny would have it, wouldn't you know it, when Jesus reached the spot, he looked up at the sycamore tree, addressed Zacchaeus by name, and told him to come down, for he intended to visit his house. The crowd was shocked that Jesus, a teacher and prophet, would sully himself by being a guest of a sinner, but it's safe to say the crowd just didn't understand. Perhaps there are people in your circle that just don't understand either. You are important to God. Zacchaeus mattered, and so do you.

Dreams do come true, but not without putting in the work. You have to make it a point to see Jesus, even if it means purposely getting in His path. Equally important is the answer to this question. What is standing between you and the manifestation of your dream? Life is not going to wait for you, and neither is time. It's time to step out on "now faith."

Love,
"the MuM"

Self - Exam Questions:

1. On a scale from 1-10, with 10 being the highest, and 1 being the lowest, where am I with what people think about me?
2. What are my true feelings about my success in life so far?
3. How am I defining success?

Faith Confessions

I decree and declare the blessings of Abraham are in my life today and always. Genesis 39 speaks of a man named Joseph, and it lets me know that even when he was a slave, he was at the top of his game because God prospered him in everything he touched. I decree and agree with God's Word when it says I am above only. I give God great praise and thanksgiving for 2 Corinthians 2:14; it is God who always causes me to triumph in Christ Jesus.

"Life is the continuous adjustment of internal relations to external relations."
- Herbert Spencer

Letter Sixteen

WHAT A DIFFERENCE A DAY MAKES

So teach us to number our days, that we may apply our hearts unto wisdom.
Psalm 90:12

Dear Beloved,

Realize that every day, all day, your help comes from God. Psalm 118:24 declares, "This is the day that the Lord has made, I will rejoice and be glad in it." How can we rejoice if we don't have joy?

Some people base their joy on things like taking a vacation, celebrating special family events, or even possessing material things. But joy cannot be predicated on a feeling. Believers can rejoice not just about what can happen, but what has happened. Jesus died for our sins; we can rejoice!

Jesus came to give us not only life, but abundant life; you can rejoice, not just on weekends or holidays, but every day that you take a breath, you can find joy. Things may have looked dim and gloomy yesterday, but when you wake up every morning, you have a brand-new opportunity not only to be blessed but to be a blessing.

Friends of mine don't stop until you attain your purpose, your dream, and your destiny. Answered prayers, fulfilled dreams, blessings and miracles await you.

Love,
"the MuM"

Self - Exam Questions:

1. How much time do I spend reminiscing about things I cannot change?
2. What small adjustments could I make to maximize my present?
3. How can I show the Lord I appreciate each day that He allows me to experience?
4. How can I make someone's day better?

Faith Confessions

Thank you, Lord, for this brand-new day. I realize there were many others with plans for this day. I also recognize that everyone that had plans are not here to see them come to fruition. Today is a gift from you. Help me to receive all of your blessings, and most of all, help me to be a blessing to others.

"Happiness is the only good. The time to be happy is now. The place to be happy is here. The way to be happy is to make others so."
- Robert Green Ingersoll

Letter Seventeen

YOU CAN DO IT TOO; IT ALL STARTS WITH YOU

**Trust in the LORD with all your heart and lean not on
your own understanding.**
Proverbs 3:5 NIV

Dear Beloved,

What is it that you have always wanted to do, but never
quite had enough courage to try? Or maybe you tried it
once, and it didn't turn out the way you planned. Right
now, just might be the time to try it again. Consider this
type of effort:

Try.

Try intentionally. Try passionately.

Try with mentorship. Try with tenacity.

Try again after setbacks.

Try with confidence.

Try even it means starting all over again.

Keep trying until your attempts bring the best results.

In other words, don't ever give up. Trying shows movement. Trying shows endeavoring. Trying shows endurance. Trying shows outcomes.

Have you realized that anything you put your mind to, you can do it? You just have to figure out what is the thing that drives you, the thing that places satisfaction in your spirit. What is the thing that you have such a passion for, that you will do for free? What is the thing that puts a smile on your face?

Whether it is to lose weight, learn a new language, get a college degree, write a blog, write a book, write a screenplay, start a non-profit, produce a podcast, build a house, start a family, restart a career, or start a ministry, it all begins in your mind.

Maybe your passion is to be a writer. Keep in mind that everyone has a voice, and everyone has a story; however, no one can tell your story the way that you can tell it. Perhaps your story is filled with highs and lows. No worries. Your story is *your* authentic story; *your* experiences and the grace extended to you from such a loving Father deserves to be told.

You have to see it by faith, believe it by faith, and work the Word by faith. Just try. Is there anything too difficult for God? No. It's not, because with God all things are possible. My truth is, I don't want to do or undertake anything without Him. He makes everything possible and profitable for His children.

For the sake of examination, let's look at a few things you cannot do without the Lord's help. You cannot breathe. You cannot communicate. You cannot form the right thoughts or counter the wrong thoughts in your mind. You can do absolutely nothing without Him. All you need is confidence in God's plan for your life, self-confidence, and a willingness to get out of your comfort zone.

If you had dared whisper in my ear five years ago that

I would be driving a commuter's van and commuting 116 miles one way from home to work two to three days a week, I would have said, "Not me." If you had dared whisper in my ear five years ago that I would seriously consider writing a book, I would probably have said again, "Not me." Getting out of your comfort zone means precisely that—departing from a place of comfort.

To move out of your comfort zone is to move into a place of unfamiliarity and there is an associated risk. It brings on its challenges because it involves entering an untrodden territory. But are you willing and ready to take the journey?

Living life without regrets just might not be your testimony. No worries; it's not mine either. However, living life does involve taking dreams, taking skills, and taking abilities to the next level by doing something about it today. Even if today only consist of writing a strategic plan with dates and conducting research. Begin today to outline your goals and be sure to incorporate your passion.

I don't know about you, but I have heard a lot of speakers speak; I have listened to a lot of teachers teach; I have heard a lot of musicians play, and I have heard a lot of preachers preach, but when these gifts are displayed with a deep passion, it makes all the difference in the world. It can bless the whole world. The excitement of a teacher with a passion for teaching goes far beyond anything the student could imagine. No matter how young or old the student is, the gift of teaching with passion is easily recognized.

When coming out of your comfort zone, your mind has to be willing to take a risk. When you think about it, you are risk-takers daily, in one way or another. You don't examine a chair before sitting. When you see a chair, even if it's in a public place, you just sit. Yes, you are counting on it being able to support your weight. Among many other things we sometimes take for granted, you expect your paycheck to be automatically deposited into your bank accounts on a specific day.

When you are traveling, you have confidence when you begin the trip, no matter the mode of transportation, no matter if it's going around the block or traveling to another continent, that you will reach your destination safely.

You can do it too; it all starts with you, your mind, and your trust level in God. Trusting in God is an excellent place to start. Have you ever placed your whole weight on something and rested in it? You can depend on God. However, you are the one that will put in the work. God will give you creative ideas and concepts, but it's up to you to execute. While putting your trust in God, always place the 3 w's into practice:

Be wise - You must seek God's wisdom in everything.

Be willing - You should always be ready to listen to and be corrected by God's Word.

Be well-positioned - Use all of your tools to get to the next dimension.

Utilize your communication to God in prayer, use the Bible as your guide, then follow God's leading. He will make your paths straight by both guiding and protecting you.

As my husband once encouraged our high school football team just before a big game with words that I now dedicate to you, my beloveds: Go hard (be passionate), go smart (be wise), and go disciplined (be self-controlled). Now go!!!

Love,
"the MuM"

Self - Exam Questions:

1. What is my strategy for not only embracing that lifelong goal, but for moving from fear to faith to get my dreams accomplished?
2. What tools has the Lord already provided for me to use?

Faith Confessions

I decree and declare that if I am willing and obedient, I will eat the good things of the land. I am fully aware that He who began a good work in me is faithful to complete it unto the day of Christ Jesus.

"Knowing is not enough; we must apply. Willing is not enough we must do."
- Johann Wolfgang von Goethe

Epilogue

Living an abundant life is the will of God. You should not have to make excuses or apologies for being blessed; favor and blessings belong to you. My prayers for you after you have read this book— (let's call the first read Round One)—are that you will be encouraged to go as many rounds as necessary while applying God's Word to every step you take.

Salvation is the first step. It is the absolute best decision you can make in life. It is a gift; however, it has to be accepted. The world is changing. The longer you have lived, the more changes you probably have noticed.

But one day, no man nor the angels know precisely when the life in which you now know, will be over. Let me encourage you to use your gifts today; please don't wait. If the dream you have inside continues to burn, don't delay, act today. Remember, small steps are okay, just step.

Should you become a risk-taker? I would vote yes on that. Go ahead and increase your trust level in God. To know God is to trust Him. He makes difficult tasks easy; after all, He breathed in us the breath of life, and we became living souls.

Greatness is in your DNA.

Represent the kingdom of God well for His glory.

Acknowledgments

I give thanks and praise to the Lord, my Savior, and my strong tower. He is truly everything to me. Initially, the prophecy came forth from my pastor, Bishop C. E. Wiley, that I would write a book, something I never expected to do in my lifetime. After receiving that word, it served as my marching orders to move into my destiny. Along with that word came these words: "It will take you some time to get it together, but you will do it." Through the ups and downs of life, there was a small, still voice that kept telling me I can do it.

I thank my very best friend in the whole world; I call him my African King, Randy M. Davis. I am so delighted that the Lord made sure he found me. Presently, this is our 40th year married, and we are enjoying God's best.

I thank God for my home training; it will never be forgotten. God blessed me with wonderful parents, C.T. and Thelma L. Cody. As I say to my mom every birthday, "Thanks for having me."

Thank God for all of my family members for their love and support. They have extraordinarily touched my life. Thanks to God for the encouragement I have received over the years, not only for this book but for every project and mission I have fulfilled.

Thank God for my church family, Blessed Hope Community, located in Prince George, Virginia. Thank God for my spiritual leaders, Bishop and Pastor Wiley. I do realize that a prophetic connection is significant before fulfilling your destiny.

The Bible says, in order to have friends you must show yourself friendly. I thank God for the friends He has placed in my life. Some friends I have met at the workplace, some on the football field, some in my neighborhood, some on our military journey, and some in other places in the community. I have lived long enough to know that people make the world go around. We all need friends.

Thank God for my mentor, Tressa Azarel Smallwood. Tressa's encouragement, patience, resourcefulness, is second to none. The "Write and Publish Like a Pro," class was so valuable to my completion of this project. The VIP club, including the powerful circle of writers, the retreats, the online classes, and the guest speakers continue to be so very valuable, to my purpose, and I highly recommend them to anyone who is contemplating this journey.

I want my family and friends to be able to say, "She made a difference." I want my enemies to say, "She made a difference." I want my unborn grandchildren and great grandchildren to say, "Thank God she took the time to pray for me and leave a legacy for our family."

Again, I thank God for the ability to express my thoughts on paper—ideas that will cause you to dig deep into your souls, with a hunger and desire to fulfill your dreams and aspirations.

About the Author

Gwendolyn Cody-Davis, who likes to be called "Cody," is a dynamic servant-leader of the Gospel of Jesus Christ. She accepted God's call into service in 1992 at Living Word Christian Fellowship in Naples, Italy. Her initial spiritual leaders during this "ministry call" were Pastors Henry Badie Jr., Henry Hawkins, and Elder Larry Morris.

She was also licensed as an evangelist at Rehoboth Baptist Church under the leadership of Dr. George G. Gaymon in 1997. Dr. and Mrs. Gaymon poured into her with encouragement and wisdom. Dr. Gaymon allowed her to implement many "first time events" in the Women's Ministry that truly motivated her as a young preacher. Presently, she serves as a licensed and ordained Elder at Blessed Hope Community (BHCC) in Prince George, Virginia, under the anointed leadership of Bishop C.E. Wiley, Senior, and Lady Amelia J. Wiley. Bishop Wiley recognized her practical and simplistic teaching style and appointed both Cody and Randy to lead the church's New Members Ministry for several years. Cody presently serves on the Board of Elders, Women's Ministry, Teen Bible Study facilitator, and she enjoys helping in whatever capacity is needed.

She is a native of Thomasville, Georgia, and a product of the Thomasville City Schools. While in high school, Cody entered into a romance, which God has since transformed into a 40-year (and counting) marriage with her best friend and husband, Randy M. Davis. Lovingly, she refers to him as her African King!

Cody is a graduate of Averett University in Danville, Virginia, where she earned a Bachelor in Business Administration in 2007. She also earned a Master of Business Administration from Averett University in 2011.

Cody's hobbies include writing, reading, decorating, shopping, listening to many genres of music, exercising, traveling, and she also enjoys Broadway plays. Her principal gifts to the body of Christ are encouraging, teaching, and motivating.

She has been privileged to speak at various women's retreats, conferences, seminars, prison ministries, and worship services in the United States and Europe. Also, Cody has broad experience as an event planner and host of spiritual retreats for women.

As a civil servant, Cody has 29 years in the Federal government. Currently, she is a Customer Account Specialist at the Defense Logistics Agency at Fort Belvoir, Virginia.

Inspirationally, the focal point of her message is for the many hurt people of the world—both saved and unsaved. She is convinced that if God has no hands, but our hands, and if He has no feet, but our feet, the question becomes, who is going to lend a hand or who is going to stoop down to pick up a hurt brother or a sister? Who has that kind of compassion and love? If not us, who? If not, now, when? Through the power of the Holy Spirit, Cody is able and willing to serve God's people.

Cody currently resides with her husband in Chester, Virginia. They are the parents of two wonderful adult sons: Ryan, and his beautiful wife, Kiandra, and Reagan, and his beautiful fiancée, Jessica.

Girly Girly

All praises to God for taking away the laws and blessing me with an awesome daughter-in-love, Kiandra.

God is a God of the encore; consequently, He has given me another amazing daughter-in-love-to-be, Jessica.

Dreams

_____

_____

_____

_____

_____

_____

_____

_____

_____

_____

_____

_____

Dreams

_____

_____

_____

_____

_____

_____

_____

_____

_____

_____

_____

_____

Dreams

_____

_____

_____

_____

_____

_____

_____

_____

_____

_____

_____

_____

Goals

_____

_____

_____

_____

_____

_____

_____

_____

_____

_____

_____

_____

Goals

_____

_____

_____

_____

_____

_____

_____

_____

_____

_____

_____

_____

Goals

_____

_____

_____

_____

_____

_____

_____

_____

_____

_____

_____